Youth Practices in Digital Arts and New Media

DOI: 10.1057/9781137475176.0001

Other Palgrave Pivot titles

Wouter Peeters, Andries De Smet, Lisa Diependaele and Sigrid Sterckx: **Climate Change and Individual Responsibility: Agency, Moral Disengagement and the Motivational Gap**

Mark Stelzner: **Economic Inequality and Policy Control in the United States**

Michelle Bayefsky and Bruce Jennings: **Regulating Preimplantation Genetic Diagnosis in the United States**

Eileen Piggot-Irvine: **Goal Pursuit in Education Using Focused Action Research**

Serenella Massidda: **Audiovisual Translation in the Digital Age: The Italian Fansubbing Phenomenon**

John Board, Alfonso Dufour, Yusuf Hartavi, Charles Sutcliffe and Stephen Wells: **Risk and Trading on London's Alternative Investment Market: The Stock Market for Smaller and Growing Companies**

Franklin G. Mixon, Jr: **Public Choice Economics and the Salem Witchcraft Hysteria**

Elisa Menicucci: **Fair Value Accounting: Key Issues Arising from the Financial Crisis**

Nicoletta Pireddu: **The Works of Claudio Magris: Temporary Homes, Mobile Identities, European Borders**

Larry Patriquin: **Economic Equality and Direct Democracy in Ancient Athens**

Antoine Pécoud: **Depoliticising Migration: Global Governance and International Migration Narratives**

Gerri Kimber: **Katherine Mansfield and the Art of the Short Story: A Literary Modernist**

C. Paul Hallwood and Thomas J. Miceli: **Maritime Piracy and its Control: An Economic Analysis**

Letizia Guglielmo and Lynée Lewis Gaillet (editors): **Contingent Faculty Publishing in Community: Case Studies for Successful Collaborations**

Katie Digan: **Places of Memory: The Case of the House of the Wannsee Conference**

Mario La Torre: **The Economics of the Audiovisual Industry: Financing TV, Film and Web**

Piero Formica: **The Role of Creative Ignorance: Portraits of Path Finders and Path Creators**

James Carson: **The Columbian Covenant: Race and the Writing of American History**

Tomasz Kamusella: **Creating Languages in Central Europe During the Last Millennium**

Imad A. Moosa and Kelly Burns: **Demystifying the Meese–Rogoff Puzzle**

DOI: 10.1057/9781137475176.0001

palgrave▸pivot

Youth Practices in Digital Arts and New Media: Learning in Formal and Informal Settings

Joanna Black

Associate Professor of Curriculum, Teaching and Learning, University of Manitoba, Canada

Juan Carlos Castro

Assistant Professor of Art Education, Concordia University, Canada

and

Ching-Chiu Lin

Postdoctoral Research Fellow, University of British Columbia, Canada

palgrave
macmillan

DOI: 10.1057/9781137475176.0001

YOUTH PRACTICES IN DIGITAL ARTS AND NEW MEDIA

First published in 2015 by
PALGRAVE MACMILLAN®
in the United States—a division of St. Martin's Press LLC,
175 Fifth Avenue, New York, NY 10010.

Where this book is distributed in the UK, Europe and the rest of the world, this is by Palgrave Macmillan, a division of Macmillan Publishers Limited, registered in England, company number 785998, of Houndmills, Basingstoke, Hampshire RG21 6XS.

Palgrave Macmillan is the global academic imprint of the above companies and has companies and representatives throughout the world.

Palgrave® and Macmillan® are registered trademarks in the United States, the United Kingdom, Europe and other countries.

ISBN: 978-1-137-47518-3 EPUB
ISBN: 978-1-137-47517-6 PDF
ISBN: 978-1-137-47516-9 Hardback

Library of Congress Cataloging-in-Publication Data is available from the Library of Congress.

A catalogue record of the book is available from the British Library.

First edition: 2015

www.palgrave.com/pivot

DOI: 10.1057/9781137475176

For all of the students, teachers, and administrators, who taught us about learning

To our families, for their love and support

DOI: 10.1057/9781137475176.0001

Contents

 DOI: 10.1057/9781137475176.0001

DOI: 10.1057/9781137475176.0001

List of Figures

DOI: 10.1057/9781137475176.0002

Acknowledgments

The editors of this book wish to acknowledge the indispensable editorial and administrative assistance of Allison Moore. Each of the authors would also like to gratefully acknowledge financial support of this research through the Social Sciences and Humanities Research Council (SSHRC) of Canada: firstly, Model New Media: Video Programs in Art Education Case Study Research (Joanna Black, principal investigator); secondly, Citizens of Tomorrow: Investigating the Impact of Community Media Arts Practice on Marginalized Urban Youth (Kit Grauer, principal investigator, Juan Carlos Castro, coinvestigator); and finally, an Insight Development Grant entitled, Youth Arts Practice as the Production of Knowledge for Community Development (Ching-Chiu Lin, principal investigator).

Notes on Contributors

Joanna Black, PhD, is Associate Professor of Art Education in the Faculty of Education and is cross-appointed as Associate Professor in the School of Art at the University of Manitoba, Winnipeg, Canada. Her research interests are on subjects of new media in education, contemporary art, digital arts pedagogy, and human rights issues. For over 30 years she has worked as an art educator, art director, museum educator, curator, art consultant, and a K-12 teacher in formal and informal settings in Canada and the United States. She has received awards from the Centre for Human Rights Research at the University of Manitoba, and the Provincial Affiliate Art Educator Award from the Canadian Society for Education through Art.

Juan Carlos Castro, PhD, is Assistant Professor of Art Education at Concordia University in Montreal, Quebec, Canada. His research focuses on the dynamics and qualities of knowing, learning, and teaching art through social and mobile media as understood through complexity thinking, network theory, and mobility studies. Prior to joining the faculty at Concordia University, Juan has taught at the University of Illinois, University of British Columbia, Johns Hopkins University, Maryland Institute College of Art, and the Burren College of Art. In 2013, he was awarded the Manuel Barkan Memorial Award from the National Art Education Association.

Kit Grauer is Professor Emerita of Art Education at the University of British Columbia, Vancouver, Canada. She is involved in art education organizations at the local,

DOI: 10.1057/9781137475176.0004

national, and international levels. Her interests include arts-based and image-based research, international issues in art education, teacher education, museum education, and art curriculum and instruction. Her current research includes Social Science and Humanities Research Grants for research creation and community-based new media education. She has received numerous awards including the Killam Teaching Excellence Award; George Cedric Metcalf Foundation Award for Excellence in Research; the Canadian Art Educator of the Year Award.

Martin Lalonde is a doctoral student and instructor in the Department of Art Education at Concordia University. His research focuses on academic motivation, social engagement of at-risk youth, participatory culture, visual culture, the development of mobile learning technologies, and new media art curricula. Prior to his time as a doctoral student, Lalonde worked as a media art and language art teacher in adult education centers for dropouts in Montreal. He is a member of the editorial board of *Vision*, the biannual journal of the Quebec art educators association (AQESAP).

Ching-Chiu Lin is a postdoctoral research fellow in the Department of Curriculum and Pedagogy at the University of British Columbia (UBC) in Vancouver, British Columbia, Canada. She is also a faculty advisor in the Teacher Education Office at UBC supervising student teaching in visual art cohorts. Lin's research interests lie in teacher mentorship, as well as issues of technology and community in art education. Lin's research and writings about art teacher education, digital-mediated arts learning, youth media, and community inquiry have been published in a number of scholarly journals and books.

DOI: 10.1057/9781137475176.0004

palgrave▸pivot

www.palgrave.com/pivot

1
Introduction

Joanna Black

Abstract: *In this chapter, ideas about youths' practices in new media are discussed that have taken place in diverse formal and informal learning environments. Definitions are provided concerning formal, informal, and nonformal sites; new media; and information communication technology. Each chapter in the book is briefly summarized, themes are examined concerning research undertaken within five Canadian learning sites, and the authors pose key questions regarding youths' digital technology and its imaginative usage in relation to concepts of creativity within our current culture.*

Keywords: art education; creative technologies; creativity; digital culture; formal learning; informal learning; in-school learning; out-of school learning; social media; youth

Black, Joanna, Juan Carlos Castro, and Ching-Chiu Lin. *Youth Practices in Digital Arts and New Media: Learning in Formal and Informal Settings.* New York: Palgrave Macmillan, 2015. DOI: 10.1057/9781137475176.0005.

The authors of this book bring together a collection of innovative research and community customs in the area of youths' practices in new media that have taken place in diverse formal and informal learning environments. It comprises descriptions of, reflections on, and examinations regarding digital mediated learning experiences, and what challenges remain to be addressed within the diverse learning communities. A focus is placed upon developing an understanding around the growing area of youth interests in digital media and arts learning in traditional and untraditional milieux in order to investigate children's digital arts practice in which the authors will identify and discuss types of learning, curricula development, knowledge sharing, distinct social contexts, and pedagogical relationships, as well as creative inquiry in school and community arts learning spaces. Furthermore, this critical discussion in relation to creativity in digital art practice will be considered in light of the recent focus on youths' participation in digital culture that affects pedagogy and social change. Formal learning environments remain important while informal learning environments are gaining increasing significance as they play a key role in the modern education of our youths. Currently, more parents are placing their children into educational community learning settings to fill in the gaps in their child's learning, add to, and complement the learning within public schools (Sefton-Green, 2013). Meanwhile, youths in our digital age are self-taught, forming communities of culture as they immerse themselves in social media outside of our classrooms.

A seminal researcher in cultural studies and media education, Buckingham (2007) suggests academics and educators turn to the model used in art education of inquiry-based, open-ended learning wherein students study art to foster self-expression, communication skills, theoretical reflection, and creativity. Using this model allows youths to explore diverse art forms and works while investigating themes such as identity and memory. He states that the implicit model "is that of the avant-garde multimedia art work" (pp. 163–164). This art education model can help educators who teach outside of the field of art education about effective teaching in the areas of new media and digital technologies in relation to cultural studies. This model is recommended because it allows students to imagine the possibilities for making digital artworks and fostering meaningful learning experiences. The authors believe that the art education practices can offer a unique (or alternative) pedagogical approach to teaching and learning with digital media for educators

DOI: 10.1057/9781137475176.0005

in other discipline areas. In this book the authors delineate ways in which art educators have designed and/or have implemented their new media programs, their curricula, and their pedagogical approaches. It is believed that the concepts presented can assist educators and administrators working with digital technologies in art and across disciplines within our public high schools and informal school settings.

There is little research that addresses the creative usage of and imaginative production of new media works in traditional schools and alternative environments (Delacruz, 2009; Gregory, 2009; Lin, 2009). Additionally, more research is definitely needed in the ways in which pedagogical practices shape learning in the context of artistic production and processes using digital technologies (Bell & Bull, 2010; Buckingham, 2009; Gregory, 2009; Halverson & Gibbons, 2009; Watts, 2008; Wilks, Cutcher, & Wilks, 2012; Willett, 2009). The authors aim to add to the much needed and crucial literature in this field by presenting empirical evidence and relevant discussion in the contexts of formal and informal learning settings.

New media usage in formal and informal settings

Formal milieux

The role of educators is vital to successful technology integration in formal school learning environments. While some devoted teachers are conducting innovative teaching with technologies, many teachers nevertheless (in art and in general subjects) are facing obstacles such as difficulty working with software and hardware, lack of training, inadequate administrational support, scanty government curricula, and high costs[1] (Bastos, 2010; Cuban, 2001; Delacruz, 2004; Gregory, 2009; Leonard & Leonard, 2006; Lu, 2005; Peppler, 2010; Roland, 2010; Watts, 2008; Wilks et al., 2012). Indeed, some teachers find it easier to pay less attention to new digital communication forms that are so ubiquitous in contemporary society (Buckingham, 2007; Choi & Piro, 2009; Willett, 2009). When educators do incorporate digital technologies, it is primarily used for mundane purposes as school-related presentations, basic computing, and acquiring information via the Internet (Buckingham, 2007; Cuban, 2001; Gregory, 2009; Lu, 2005; Peppler, 2010; Roland, 2010). In essence, technology is predominantly employed for banal, commonplace uses

DOI: 10.1057/9781137475176.0005

such as replacing notebooks, chalkboards, and libraries in our public schools, and a great deal of money has been spent on it (Leonard & Leonard, 2006). Critics often discuss school educators' lack of knowledge regarding ways teachers integrate technologies effectively in classrooms in order to address concerns of student disenchantment and youth disengagement in education (Jenkins, 2009; Prensky, 2010).

Researchers observe that young people's daily encounter with digital technologies is often in direct contrast to schooling practices (Buckingham, 2007; Castro, Sinner, & Grauer, 2010; Gude, 2007; Prensky, 2010, Roland, 2010). There is often a gaping divide between the savvy ways in which our youths use media outside of school in their everyday digital lives versus the structured, controlled, and often stilted ways it is regularly used within schools (Clark, Logan, Luckin, Mee, & Oliver, 2009). Clark and his colleagues write, "... school institutions appear to be slow to realize the potential of collaborative, communicative interactions, and the open and flexible potentials of learning 'beyond the classroom walls'" (p. 68).

Some researchers such as Davidson and Goldberg (2012) write about what they perceive as oppression of learning in formal settings and call for a change within these institutions in light of emerging information communication technology (ICT) and its potential for participatory and digital learning. Nevertheless, a few art educators within public schools have overcome these obstacles, and engaged in innovative practices making connections outside of formal learning environments within the larger community. These new media programs engage youth, offer strategies for motivating learners, and enable young people to produce and excel in media production. There is scant detailed, thick description about the ways in which art teachers teach with technologies creatively in the classrooms. Revealing such examples is important for policy makers and teachers in order to understand the potential of effective pedagogical approaches and curricula development using new media in public schools (Delacruz, 2004, 2009). How do teachers effectively teach with digital technologies in their classrooms? Scholars have been pointing to the need for more descriptive studies in order to address the above question (Browning, 2006; Darts, 2007; Flood & Bamford, 2007; Gadsden, 2008; Gregory, 2009; Jewitt, 2008; Taylor, 2007). It is recommended that educators need to consider the kinds of skills and knowledge young learners bring to these formal milieux. As Wilks et al. (2012) suggest, the "reality is that in many art classrooms the possibilities have not yet

DOI: 10.1057/9781137475176.0005

been embraced. Art educators will need assistance to develop a vision for planning and interpretation of ICT [Information Communication Technologies] in their curricula" (p. 64). Finally, it is advised that researchers need to examine the transferability of skills between formal and informal settings (Clark et al., 2009) in order to help young people navigate the complexity of a constantly changing world.

Informal milieux

Attention needs to be given to the qualities of informal learning spaces as they are increasingly present in the digital practices of youth and are essential to engaging young people from socially and culturally diverse backgrounds. It is often recorded that informal learning is undertaken by the students who are highly motivated, eager to learn, and find informal learning to be exciting, flexible, organic, versatile, instantaneous, and diverse (Davidson & Goldberg, 2012; Gunga & Ricketts, 2008; Lin & Mendoza, 2014). Sefton-Green (2013) notes that there is not a great deal of research pertaining to informal learning and ICT usage, suggesting that researchers should examine "How in-formal learning developed in the home, by one's self or as part of an interest-driven community [and] might be valorized and further developed through not-school experiences" (p. 74). Also of significance are youths' learning and skill development undertaken at home, in domestic settings, and created for personal use in their own *life world*. This is illustrated in Freedman, Heijnen, Kallio-Tavin, Kárpáti, and Papp's (2013) international research study that identified the growing occurrence of youth who form visual culture learning communities outside of formal and informal education programs.

Integrating ICT within society has caused sites of informal learning to gain importance as many learn about ICT outside the classroom (Gunga & Ricketts, 2008). Researchers are finding that instructors in informal learning contexts play a key role as they assist learners taking part in self-determined activities. Sefton-Green (2013) specifically addresses the scant research in this area particularly in recent years. However, he does provide a detailed description of two models undertaken over 30 years ago in Britain and the United States (pp. 41–51).

As informal learning in ICT becomes more dominant, education in these sites of learning is often not as controlled (Gunga & Ricketts, 2008; Sefton-Green, 2013). In Canadian contexts, many researchers

DOI: 10.1057/9781137475176.0005

have explored how informal educational sites use various art forms and/or digital media to facilitate and enrich inquiry for underrepresented young people beyond school settings (Darts, 2007; Irwin & Kindler, 1999; Poyntz, 2009; Sinner, 2010; Winters, Rogers, & Schofield, 2006). Some describe the effectiveness of community arts programming regarding integrating social services (Browne, 2003), preventing behavioral problems (Wright et al., 2006), developing general skill sets (Fix & Sivak, 2007), literacy proficiency (Rogers, 2010), and fostering multicultural awareness (Kuly, Stewart, & Dudley, 2005) for children and youth in multiethnic communities. Others consider digital-mediated arts production, such as film and digital photography, as a source for artistic expression and a tool of empowerment for immigrant and refugee youth (Lui, 2005) and marginalized teen girls (Levy & Weber, 2011). Although this literature indicates informal learning sites serve as a public space to reach various social needs for youth on the margins, such an intentional learning outcome has been critiqued, suggesting that young people hold a passive relationship to media, assuming that media shape their mind and behavior (Goldman, Booker, & McDermott, 2008). What is absent from this research literature is a contemporary understanding of how digital technologies are creating opportunities for new forms of artistic expression and communication for young people in the context of community-based programming. Often digital education in informal learning lacks *creative* learner development not only in media and multimodal literacies but also in the development of *criticality* that is currently being dominated by endless banal entertainment and mundane communication needs (Buckingham, 2007; Clark et al., 2009).

There is an apparent shift in the literature within the last 25 years regarding informal learning settings and ICT usages. This alteration manifests itself in three ways: (1) a current emphasis is on the *individual* versus a past emphasis situated within *community*; (2) a present focus is on *economics* rather than an earlier one positioned within *social values*; and (3) a contemporary movement pertains to "*pedagogicizing*" everyday life versus formerly valuing outside activities for themselves and their inherent worth (Sefton-Green, 2013, pp. 78–79).

Scholarly interest in informal learning and digital media has grown progressively as researchers note its impact upon learners (Colley, Hodkinson, & Malcolm, 2003). In recent years research into young people's digital participation in sites of informal learning has increased (Burn, 2009; Colley et al., 2003; Sefton-Green, 2014), as evidenced in the

DOI: 10.1057/9781137475176.0005

variety of research undertaken in diverse disciplines ranging from music (Jenkins, 2011) and outdoor education (O'Mahony, 2010) to music, science (Anastopoulou, Sharples, Ainsworth, Crook, O'Malley & Wright, 2014), and media studies (Goodman, 2005; Sefton-Green, 2013).

Definitions of terms

New media

New media technology includes the study of process, production, and analysis of a variety of contemporary digital art forms. The authors refer to Rush (2005) and his discussion in his book, entitled *New Media in Art*:

> It would be difficult to exaggerate the effect of digital technology on the production of art in the twenty-first century. From digitally altered photographs to rapid prototyped sculptures to quantum (cameraless) movies, the use of digital technology is pervasive...the inexorable march of the world toward a digital (or computerized) culture has included art in its step. (p. 180)

Rush discusses new media in relation to the following categories including computer art, Internet art, video installation, media and performance, digital photography, digital video, sound art, experimental sculpture, and other digital interactive art forms (2005). In this book the authors discuss new media specifically pertaining to film, animation, digital imaging, web-based artwork, audio productions, and video art.

Information and Communication Technology

ICT is the study of tools, resources, and applications of computer digital devices, information, and communications. The authors use this term in this book to indicate digital systems and productions to collect, store, use, share, inform, create, communicate, and disseminate digital information locally, nationally, and internationally.

Formal learning settings

In recent decades many researchers have addressed issues of differentiation between concepts of formal learning and informal learning (Beckett & Hager, 2013; Billett, 2002; Colley et al., 2003; Edwards, Nicoll, Solomon, & Usher, 2013; Eraut, 2000; Hager & Halliday, 2006; Hodkinson & Hodkinson, 2004). Colley and her colleagues (2003) note there is a lack

DOI: 10.1057/9781137475176.0005

of agreement in terms of defining these areas, and Sefton-Green (2013) suggests that these terms are complex: consequently, the authors will proceed to define our terms pertaining to our text.

It is important to first articulate what **formal learning** is, which is often called *school education* or compulsory mass schooling (Anastopoulou et al., 2014; Sefton-Green, 2013). This consists of a series of structured curricula that occur within education systems organized hierarchically from primary to university levels (Bevan & Dillon, 2010; Clark et al., 2009; Coombs & Ahmed, 1974; Erstad, 2012; Fordham, 1993; Jenkins, 2011; Scheerens, 2009a, 2009b). Characteristics of formal education include certification, constrained practicalities, time specifications, and strict organizational features overseen by governmental controls within public education (Gunga & Ricketts, 2008; Jenkins, 2011). Teachers working within formal learning environments must acquire requisite certification. Other aspects involve continuing education, vocational training, and specialized technical programs. These curricula occur within government recognized schools, colleges, and training centers where attendance is usually mandated by law and where learning is measured through standardized means (Hager & Halliday, 2009).

Informal learning settings

Falling under the boundaries of **informal learning** is *everyday learning* and *lifelong learning* which are often defined in opposition to formal learning because these include learning through the daily activities of an individual. In simple terms this means "not school" within institutions as defined by Sefton-Green (2013) or learning from daily *life worlds*. Informal learning is considered more organic, less structured, contextualized, and based on activities and experiences rooted in the lives of learners. The act of learning something is initiated by learners rather than instructors (Beckett & Hager, 2013). In the context of informal education, the learner is not always aware that learning occurs for it is often subconscious (Gunga & Ricketts, 2008) and therefore becomes difficult to determine the exact learning outcomes of activities. However, the learner operates with the freedom to determine the subject and methods of inquiry.

Informal education includes everything that falls outside the formal structures of formal learning. It can take place in the domestic household, neighborhood, community, within given peer groups, religious institutions, after-school and community organizations, employment,

DOI: 10.1057/9781137475176.0005

recreation, and when it engages learners in traditional and digital media (Buckingham, 2011; Gunga & Ricketts, 2008; Hannigan, 2012). Informal learning occurs, for example, when individuals watch television science documentaries, engage in museum exhibitions, visit libraries, and take lessons at community centers (Bevan & Dillon, 2010; Heath, 2001). In these sites learners pursue development of ideas and skills they desire to acquire and improve upon, which is called a "third arena of learning" (Heath, 2001, p. 10). Within these informal settings teaching and learning are not undertaken within constricting boundaries of strict regulations and rigidity but rather, are often extremely flexible and versatile (Gunga & Ricketts, 2008).

Nonformal learning

La Belle (1982) states that informal learning can occur in formal settings and vice versa. This highlights the importance of what is called nonformal educational contexts in relationship to formal settings (Hager & Halliday, 2006). Nonformal education is halfway between the formal and informal (Colley et al., 2003). It differs from formal and informal education because it is learning activity that occurs inside the formal framework of an official educational institution, yet does not follow the prescribed and structured activities dictated by the institution (Coombs & Ahmed, 1974; Fordham, 1993). One such example is home schooling where informal settings are sites of learning within traditional schooling.

A discussion of formal, informal, and nonformal environments

Learning context and environment play a central role in the differentiation between formal, informal, and nonformal education. Areas of study are plentiful in relation to informal and formal learning, particularly in the context of emerging digital technologies. Recently, researchers are noting emerging problems between informal and formal learning sites. On the one hand, it is observed that the bridging of informal and formal learning environments currently has seemingly insurmountable divisions (Bevan & Dillon, 2010). There is often a disconnection, for instance, apparent between formal learning and informal learning pertaining to the examination of the daily life of learners in subjects such

DOI: 10.1057/9781137475176.0005

as science, but it is more often apparent in digital technologies' usage and applications (Anastopoulou et al., 2014; O'Mahony, 2010). On the other hand, other researchers observe that various forms of youths' education between formal and informal in today's society are indeed interconnecting in ways not imaged as informal education is emerging as powerful, forceful, influential, abundant, and often uncontrolled, particularly in relation to ICT (Gunga & Ricketts, 2008).

As stated earlier, the gap between learners' media usage personally inside and outside of school is increasing and problematic (Erstad, 2012). Clark and his colleagues (2009) have termed this *digital dissonance*, and they corroborate that it is this chasm that is growing and critical: they advise further study as it remains unsettled and problematic. They also find that particularly restrictive, regulatory, stringent formal school rules exist within formal institutions, and while learners perceive the positive potential of digital usage, educators are not comprehending this—nor are they understanding its creative and educative potentials. Davidson and Goldberg (2012) write about what they perceive as the excitement in digital learning within informal settings versus mundane routinization within formal institutions. Clark et al. (2009) pose the important question: "If young people *are* acquiring new and valuable skills sets in and through their interactions with technologies, how can these usefully be introduced to more specific settings such as formal education?" (p. 57). Digital learning within informal/formal settings will be discussed in this book in relation to five research sites across Canada.

Discussion of the book

In Chapter 2, Ching-Chiu Lin discusses the rise of emerging technologies and its connection to economics and creativity. Creativity in relation to learning through digital media is discussed in terms of social practice and collective endeavors. She notes that the growing public interest in coupling creativity to the economy indicates that education has become a site of contestation for promoting market-driven values, thus emphasizing product over process to advance industry and career concerns. In this chapter Lin specifically describes a Frames Film Project (Frames) for underrepresented youth ages 16–24 situated in a community organization in Vancouver, British Columbia. Frames pedagogical, curricula, and professional approaches are discussed as a unique perspective

DOI: 10.1057/9781137475176.0005

to understand the changing landscape of community youth media programs. Noted are different aims of the administrators and teachers/professional artists who, on the one hand, endeavor to prepare students for potential employments and life skills, while on the other hand, intend to develop youths' voices in order to express ways in which commercial, cultural, societal, and governmental structures are affecting their lives.

The dichotomy between students' unconfined, uncontrolled digital practices outside of school and the restrained, constricted, digital world inside many traditional school practices, creates *digital dissonance* (Clark et al., 2009) and is evident in the research work discussed by Martin Lalonde and Juan Carlos Castro in Chapter 3. The authors examine the Montreal area community arts center, Maison Kekpart, an arts center for at-risk youths: Kekpart's mission is to reengage teenagers and young adults with learning through the study of creative social media processes and production. Fostering youths' responsible and professional ways of handling new media is nurtured in this informal setting through intrinsic motivation and through training in digital imaging, sound design, and video production. Key to Maison Kekpart's program are youths' use of social media as self-representation, identity construction, and social engagement and for co-constructions of knowledge within shared and public creative communities.

Manitoba, located in the prairies of central Canada, is the site of two formal learning environments examined by Joanna Black in Chapter 4. One school, Orangeville Collegiate Institute, has a new media program for middle class economically privileged secondary students, and the other school, Applewood Alternative High School, has a new media program for a large at-risk Aboriginal student population. Objectives in both programs are to teach new media as art and to foster student creativity. Educators' key aims are similar to both programs: to educate students in life skills and community building practices. The author particularly examines the importance of educators' autonomy involved in teaching new media so that the rigidity of traditional schooling is broken down in order to create strong curricula and flexible pedagogical approaches within traditional schools.

In Chapter 5, Ching-Chiu Lin and Kit Grauer examine a new media program offered by The Gulf Islands Film and Television School (GIFTS) located in British Columbia, on the west coast of Canada. Highlighted are the digital engagements of youths and their creative practices concerning both the process and products of film/video production. At GIFTS,

DOI: 10.1057/9781137475176.0005

educators are placed in the role of facilitators, and many are professionals working in the film industry. Professionalism, social collaboration, sense of collective engagement, and creative practices are fostered through this intensive one-week program in a unique learning environment. The authors discuss time constraints, given this tight schedule, which break down rigid, formal, learning patterns. Importantly, rather than emphasizing digital technologies' capacity as a tool for media production, the authors discuss the significance of youth engagement as a form of social practice.

Conclusion

In the book particular emphasis is placed on the relationship regarding youths' digital culture in connection to creativity, its correlation to technology, and the potential for fostering youths' imagination. Rather than conduct another study in which researchers pit formal against information education, the authors examine ways in which new media pedagogical approaches in traditional education and in alternative settings can inform each other, and can inform general practice within art education and extend to other disciplines. The prevalent view is that informal and formal are separate (Colley et al., 2003). Colley recognizes that there is an interrelationship which varies within each setting and states that the challenge is to recognize these. Moreover, Sefton-Green (2013) acknowledges that context of learning in informal learning environments can indeed take place in the more formal ones (pp. 21–22). As recommended by Colley et al. (2003), the authors of this study do not make the claim that either formal or informal learning is superior.

Many questions are posed. Can we learn from excellence in education in both informal and formal learning environments? Do these diverse educational experiences have pedagogical and curricula commonalities? Is there a flow between the formal and informal learning environments? Can we harness the knowledge students bring from their personal lives into learning and education within formal and informal contexts? And finally, do educators in formal and informal learning environments understand and use new media creatively and critically and see its potentials within their particular milieu? The authors of this study seek to find out whether there are unproscriptive and flexible models, both in formal and informal settings, that have realized this potential. Erstad's

DOI: 10.1057/9781137475176.0005

(2012, pp. 28, 40) recommendation is employed that we move beyond the practice of pitting informal and formal setting against one another to examine which is better. We need to provide an alternative discourse in order to bridge a gap between these divided spaces so that contemporary education is reorganized and reshaped. This, the author states, requires substantial support through research in order to realize new potentials for 21st century education. We hope to move beyond and create connections between these learning sites.

Note

1 Refer to Black's thesis (2002) for a more comprehensive list of obstacles teachers confront in using digital technologies within public schools. Even though the research was undertaken over a decade ago these reasons remain.

References

Anastopoulou, S., Sharples, M., Ainsworth, S., Crook, C., O'Malley, C. & Wright, M. (2014). Creating personal meaning through technology-supported science inquiry learning across formal and informal settings. *International Journal of Science Education, 34*(2), 251–273, DOI: 10.1080/09500693.2011.569958.

Bastos, F. (2010). New media art education. *Art Education, 63*(1), 4–5.

Beckett, D. & Hager, P. (2013). *Life, Work and Learning: Practice in Postmodernity*. New York: Taylor & Francis.

Bell, L. & Bull, G. (2010). Digital video and teaching. *Contemporary Issues in Technology and Teacher Education, 10*(1), 1–6.

Bevan, B. & Dillon, J. (2010). Broadening views of learning: developing educators for the 21st century through an international research partnership at the Exploratorium and King's College London. *The New Educator, 6*, 167–180.

Billett, S. (2002). Critiquing workplace learning discourses: participation and continuity at work. *Studies in the Education of Adults, 34*(1), 56–67.

Black, J. (2002). Topsy-turvy teacher-student relationships: an examination of digital multimedia teaching and learning (Doctoral dissertation, University of Toronto, 2002). *Dissertation Abstracts International, 63*, 6.

Browne, G. (2003). Integrated service delivery: more effective and less expensive. *Ideas That Matter* 2(3). Retrieved from http://www.ideasthatmatter.com/quarterly/itm-2-3/vol2no3.pdf.

Browning, C. (2006). Digital applications in elementary visual arts: a case study in Ontario and Newfoundland schools. *Canadian Review of Art Education, 33*, 25–41.

Buckingham, D. (2007). *Beyond Technology: Children's Learning in the Age of Digital Culture*. Cambridge, England: Polity Press.

Buckingham, D. (2009). A commonplace art? Understanding amateur media productions. In D. Buckingham, & R. Willett (Eds), *Video cultures: media technology and everyday creativity* (pp. 23–50). New York, NY: Palgrave Macmillan.

Buckingham, D. (2011). Youth media production in the digital age: some reflections—and a few provocations. In J. Fisherkeller (Ed.), *International Perspectives on Youth Media: Cultures of Production and Education* (pp. 375–379). New York, NY: Peter Lang Publishing.

Burn, A. (2009). *Making New Media: Creative Production and Digital Literacies*. New York, NY: Peter Lang Publishing.

Castro, J. C., Sinner, A. & Grauer, K. (2010). New media arts education: how community based programs can reshape teaching and learning in the age of Web 2.0. In G. Sweeny (Ed.), *Inter/Actions/Inter/Sections: Art Education in a Digital Visual Culture* (pp. 80–89). Reston, VA: National Art Education Association Publication.

Choi, H. & Piro, J. M. (2009). Expanding arts education in a digital age. *Arts Education Policy Review, 110*(3), 27–34.

Clark, W., Logan, K., Luckin, R., Mee, A. & Oliver, M. (2009). Beyond Web 2.0: mapping technology landscapes of young learners. *Journal of Computer Assisted Learning, 25*, 56–69.

Colley, H., Hodkinson, P. & Malcolm, J. (2003). Understanding informality and formality in learning. *Adults Learning, 15*(3), 7–9.

Coombs, P. H. & Ahmed, M. (1974). *Attacking Rural Poverty: How Nonformal Education Can Help*. Baltimore, MD: Johns Hopkins University Press.

Cuban, L. (2001). *Oversold & Underused: Computers in the Classroom*. Cambridge, MA: Harvard University Press.

Darts, D. (2007). Learning through new eyes: rethinking media, popular culture and art education. In R. Irwin, K. Grauer, & M. Emme (Eds),

DOI: 10.1057/9781137475176.0005

Revisions: Readings in Canadian Art Teacher Education. Thunder Bay, Ontario: Canadian Society for Education through Art.

Davidson, C. & Goldberg, D. (2012). Our digital age: implications for learning and its (online) institutions. *E-Learning and Digital Media, 9*(3), 249–266.

Delacruz, E. (2004). Teachers' working conditions and the unmet promise of technology. *Studies in Art Education, 46*(1), 6–19.

Delacruz, E. (2009). Art education aims in the age of new media: moving toward global civil society. *Art Education, 62*(5), 13–17.

Edwards, R., Nicoll, K., Solomon, N. & Usher, R. (2013). *Rhetoric and Educational Discourse: Persuasive Texts.* New York, NY: Taylor & Francis.

Eraut, M. (2000). Non-formal learning and tacit knowledge in professional work. *British Journal of Educational Psychology, 70*(1), 113–136.

Erstad, O. (2012). The learning lives of digital youth – beyond the formal and informal. *Oxford Review of Education, 38*(1), 25–43.

Fix, E. & Sivak, N. (2007). The growing case for youth engagement through culture. *Our Diverse Cities*, (Fall), 145–151.

Flood, A. & Bamford, A. (2007). Manipulation, simulation, stimulation: the role of art education in the digital age. *International Journal of Education through Art, 3*(2), 91–102.

Fordham, P. E. (1993). *Informal, Non-Formal and Formal Education Programmes in YMCA George Williams College ICE301 Lifelong Learning Unit 2*. London: YMCA George Williams College.

Freedman, K., Heijnen, E., Kallio-Tavin, M., Kárpáti, A. & Papp, L. (2013). Visual culture learning communities: how and what students come to know in informal art groups. *Studies in Art Education, 54*(2), 103–115.

Gadsden, V. (2008). The arts and education: knowledge, generation, and pedagogy. *Review of Research in Education, 32*, 29–61.

Goldman, S. Booker, A. & McDermott, M. (2008). Mixing the digital, social, and cultural: learning, identity, and agency in youth participation. In D. Buckingham (Ed.), *Youth, Identity, and Digital Media* (pp. 185–206). Cambridge: The MIT Press.

Goodman, S. (2005). The practice and principles of teaching critical literacy at the educational video center. In G. Schwarz & P. Brown (Eds), *Media Literacy: Transforming Curriculum and Teaching* (pp. 206–228). Malden, MA: National Society for the Study of Education.

DOI: 10.1057/9781137475176.0005

Gregory, D. (2009). Boxes with fire: wisely integrating learning technologies into the art classroom. *Art Education, 62*(3), 47–54.

Gude, O. (2007). Principles of possibility: consideration for a 21st century art & culture curriculum. *Art Education, 60*(1), 6–17.

Gunga, S. & Ricketts, I. (2008). The prospects for e-learning revolution in education: a philosophical analysis. *Educational Philosophy and Theory, 40*(2), 294–314.

Hager, P. J. & Halliday, J. (2006). *Recovering Informal Learning Wisdom, Judgment and Community.* Dordrecht: Springer. Retrieved from http://public.eblib.com/choice/ publicfullrecord.aspx?p=301811.

Halverson, E. & Gibbons, D. (2009). "Key Moments" as pedagogical windows into the video production process. *Journal of Computing in Teacher Education, 26*(2), 69–74.

Hannigan, S. (2012). Turning community stories into community art. *International Journal of Education Through Art, 8*(2), 135–150.

Heath, S. (2001). Three's not a crowd: plans, roles, and focus. *Educational Researcher, 30*(7), 10–17.

Hodkinson, P. & Hodkinson, H. (2004). The complexities of workplace learning. In H. Rainbird, A. Fuller, & A. Munro (Eds), *Workplace Learning in Context* (pp. 259–275). London: Routledge.

Irwin, R. & Kindler, A. (Eds). (1999). *Beyond the School: Community and Institutional Partnerships in Art Education.* Reston, VA: The National Art Education Association.

Jenkins, H. (2009). *Confronting the Challenges of Participatory Culture: Media Education for the 21st Century.* Cambridge, MA: MIT Press.

Jenkins, P. (2011). Formal and informal music educational practices. *Philosophy of Music Education Review, 19*(2), 179–197.

Jewitt, C. (2008). Multimodality and literacy in school classrooms. *Review of Research in Education, 32*, 241–267.

Kuly, M. Stewart, E. & Dudley, M. (2005). *Enhancing Cultural Capital: The Arts and Community Development in Winnipeg.* Winnipeg: Institute of Urban Studies at the University of Winnipeg.

La Belle, T. J. (1982). Formal, nonformal and informal education: a holistic perspective on lifelong learning. *International Review of Education, 28*(2), 159–175.

Leonard, L. & Leonard, P. (2006, Winter). Leadership for technology integration: computing the reality. *The Alberta Journal of Educational Research, 52*(4), 212–224.

DOI: 10.1057/9781137475176.0005

Levy, L. & Weber, S. (2011). Teenmom.ca, a community arts based new media empowerment project for teenage mothers. *Studies in Art Education, 52*(4), 292–309.

Lin, C. (2009). Beyond visual literacy competencies: teaching and learning art with technology in the global age. In E. Delacruz, A. Arnold, A. Kuo, & M. Parsons (Eds), *Globalization, Art, and Education* (pp. 198–204). Reston, VA: National Art Education Association.

Lin, C. & Mendoza, K. (2014). Youth interests and digital media: 4-H podcasting program in Urbana Middle School. In B. Bruce, A. Bishop, & N. Budhathoki (Eds), *Youth Community Inquiry: New Media for Community and Personal Growth. Using New Media for Community Building and Personal Growth* (pp. 17–22). New York, NY: Peter Lang Publishing.

Lu, Li-Fen. (2005). Pre-service art teacher negative attitudes and perceptions of computer-generated art imagery: recommendations for pre-service art education programs. *Visual Arts Research, 31*(1), 89–102

Lui, J. (2005). Redefining Canadian: a participatory filmmaking, action research project with immigrant and refugee youth. Unpublished Master Thesis, Simon Fraser University.

O'Mahony, T. K. (2010). *Connecting Formal and Informal Learning Experiences* (Doctoral dissertation, University of Washington). Retrieved from ProQuest Dissertations and Theses database (UMI No. 964183276).

Peppler, K. (2010). Media arts: art education for a digital age. *Teachers College Record, 112*(6), 2118–2153.

Poyntz, S. (2009). "On behalf of a shared world": Arendtian politics in a culture of youth media production. *Review of Education, Pedagogy and Cultural Studies, 31*(4), 365–386.

Prensky, M. (2010). *Teaching Digital Natives: Partnering for Real Learning.* Thousand Oaks, CA: Corwin/Sage Ltd.

Rogers, T. (2010). Theorizing media productions as complex literacy performances among youth in and out of schools. In D. Pullen & D. Cole (Eds), *Multiliteracies and Technology Enhanced Education: Social Practice and the Global Classroom* (pp. 133–146). Hershey, PA: IGI Global Snippet.

Roland, C. (2010). Preparing art teachers to teach in a new digital landscape. *Art Education, 63*(1), 17–24.

Rush, M. (2005). *New Media in Art.* New York, NY: Thames and Hudson.

DOI: 10.1057/9781137475176.0005

Scheerens, J. (2009a). Aims and scope of the study. In J. Scheerens (Ed.), *Informal Learning of Active Citizenship at School: Vol. 14* (pp. 1–10). Dordrecht, The Netherlands: Springer Netherlands.

Scheerens, J. (Ed.). (2009b). *Informal Learning of Active Citizenship at School: Vol. 14*. Dordrecht, The Netherlands: Springer. Retrieved from http://link.springer.com/10.1007/978-1-4020-9621-1.

Sefton-Green, J. (2013). *Learning a Not-School: A Review of Study, Theory and Advocacy for Education in Non-Formal Settings*. Cambridge, MA: MIT Press.

Sefton-Green, J. (2014). From "othering" to incorporation: the dilemmas of crossing informal and formal learning boundaries. In K. Sanford, T. Rogers, and M. Kendrick (Eds), *Everyday Youth Literacies: Critical Perspectives for New Times* (pp. 175–189). Singapore: Springer.

Sinner, A. (2010). Digital storytelling as art practice: a case of informal learning. *Arts and Learning Research Journal, 26*(10), 1–19.

Taylor, P. (2007). Mediating art education: digital kids, art and technology. *Visual Arts Research, 22*(65), 84–95.

Watts, J. K. (2008). Teaching digital media as an art class: a search to define a curriculum (Doctoral Dissertation). Retrieved from ProQuest Dissertations and Theses database (UMI No. 3341339).

Wilks, J., Cutcher, A., & Wilks, S. (2012). Digital technology in the visual arts classroom: an [un]easy partnership. *Studies in Art Education, 54*(1), 54–65.

Willett, R. (2009). Young people's video productions as new sites of learning. In V. Carrington &M. Robinson (Eds), *Digital Literacies: Social Learning and Classroom Practices* (pp. 13–26). Thousand Oaks, CA: Sage Publications.

Winters, K., Rogers, T., Schofield, A. (2006). "The Antigone Project: exploring the imaginative, active, and social dimensions of drama, print literacy, and media." In J. Schneider, T. Crumpler, & T. Rogers (Eds). *Process Drama: An Educational Tool for Developing Multiple Literacies*. Portsmouth, NH: Heinemann.

DOI: 10.1057/9781137475176.0005

2

Economic, Social, and Personal Aspects of Educating for Creativity: A Study of a Community-Based Youth Media Arts Program

Ching-Chiu Lin

Abstract: *This chapter is about the growing impact of an economic rationale for the relationship between creativity and learning, especially in the context of community-based youth media arts practices. By presenting a unique case and discussion of Frames Film Project, a community-based media program serving youth dealing with mental health issues and/or substance abuse in Vancouver, British Columbia, I provide perspectives on ways of understanding, conceptualizing, and interpreting what it means to be a creative learner in the 21st century, as well as insight into how a youth program operates under economically challenging conditions.*

Keywords: art education; community development; creativity; media education; youth arts practice

Black, Joanna, Juan Carlos Castro, and Ching-Chiu Lin. *Youth Practices in Digital Arts and New Media: Learning in Formal and Informal Settings.* New York: Palgrave Macmillan, 2015. DOI: 10.1057/9781137475176.0006.

Youth media arts practice and digital participation is an interdisciplinary research area, as making and consuming digital media have become part of the lives of young people. Central to the topic are the educational strategies for enabling young people's creative practices in response to the emergence of digital technologies. This reflects the current public discourse on realizing the economic benefits and values that are generated from creative practices and new digital technologies (Harris, 2014; Hesmondhalgh, 2007; Throsby, 2001). In this chapter, I aim to address the growing impact of this economic rationale in the context of community-based youth media arts practices. This is examined through the discussion of a study of a community-based media program serving youth dealing with mental health issues and/or substance abuse in Vancouver, British Columbia. With economic justification so powerful in shaping education in the 21st century, I hope to provide a perspective on the present public and educational discourses about creative and digital endeavors with a particular focus on youth and community development. I ask: What are the possible relationships between creativity and learning in youth media programs? What is an understanding of creativity that is not necessarily tied to an economic justification in young people's media arts practice and digital participation? My intention is to provide educators and teachers a situated understanding of creativity and learning that addresses social, economic, and cultural conditions. Nonetheless, I do not mean either to promote or to reject the impact of neoliberalism on youth media arts practices. Instead, my aim is to acknowledge the changing social and economic climate and identify pedagogical implementations for thinking beyond it.

Why creativity now?

Over the past 30 years, research and practice in creativity have attracted attention from researchers, educators, business leaders, policy makers, and the general public (Craft, 2011; Jagodzinski, 2013; Zimmerman, 2009). This is because creativity is increasingly seen as a critical component across the broader economy (Chan & Thomas, 2013; Jones, 2012). Nevertheless, creativity is a fluid concept that continuously changes to meet society's needs and has varied interpretations and connotations across disciplines. For example, in the field of art education, conceptions of creativity have evolved over time and manifested as artistic

DOI: 10.1057/9781137475176.0006

talent, self-expression, or a social construct in response to changes in students' aesthetic and artistic development, educational paradigms, emerging digital technologies, and the social contexts of students' lives.[1] In the recent discourse of framing creativity as an economic imperative, it is understood, according to Jones (2011), as "a mode of being, a set of dispositions involving qualities such as initiative, innovativeness, commitment, patience and concentration, whose stimulus and justification lay primarily in economic life" (p. 24). In line with this discourse is the creativity–imagination–innovation nexus, in which advocates maintain that creativity steers the possibilities of imagination that, in turn, may spark innovation for productivity since the workforce is changing rapidly with technological change. Such logic underlines "a sequential link between individual capabilities and joint outcomes of wider societal and economic significance" (Drotner, 2011, p. 73). In turn, the growing interest in linking creativity to economic justification has generated a resurgence of claims that education is the key to fostering creative behaviors. Bringing education into this equation reflects a political ideology of neoliberalism that promotes market-driven educational values focusing on competitiveness, individualism, and standardization (Couldry, 2010; Giroux, 2011; Rogers, 2013).[2]

At the same time, digital-mediated arts practices (e.g., film, computer animation, digital photography, video game art, and web design) have emerged as an avenue for young people to engage, interpret, and participate in an increasingly complex world. As media arts enable ways of representing knowledge, voice, and experience, digital media production programs for youth are increasingly recognized as an effective means of building individual skills, promoting community engagement, and providing broader social values (Jenkins, 2008; Lin & Bruce, 2013; Peppler & Solomou, 2011; Poyntz, 2009; Sope, 2006). Such programs offer a space outside of schools that enable young people to foster a sense of self-advocacy, empowerment, and resilience. Youth media arts practices offer a means for responding to how social, economic, cultural, and political structures affect their lives, and to help young people draw connections to individuals and their communities through the production process (Fisherkeller, 2011, 2013; Hull & Nelson, 2010; Lacy, 2010). As Sefton-Green (2011) pinpoints, we are entering an era in digital culture that pays significant attention to "what young people actually make" (p. 249). Thus, there are more discourses related to youth-made media that emphasize forms, production values, techniques, and communication

DOI: 10.1057/9781137475176.0006

effectiveness. Yet, because of economic values of digital production concerning employment, the common impression of youth participation in digital culture and their creative media arts practices often focuses on the quality of end products rather than the contextual process of learning. Often, forms of youth media arts production are optimistically appraised by their commodity value in search of connections to the industries striving for creativity, innovation and digital competence (Harris, 2014; Osborne, 2003). As a consequence, this popularity of youth media production is aligned with a "product-oriented conception of creativity" driven by economic interests that "has as an emphasis on individuality, a strong work ethic, and belief that progress is always for the betterment of society" (Zimmerman, 2009, p. 391). This notion of creativity is affiliated with discussion around Richard Florida's (2002) model of the "creative class" that signals "the emergence of a new social type that is endowed with both cultural and creative capital" (Darras, 2011, p. 94). This discourse justifies a job training scheme for youth media programs as film and video are seen as creative products in which "economic properties" (Caves, 2000, p. 2) are embedded. While such an approach encourages youth to gain perspectives on career preparation, it also classifies them as vulnerable "citizens/patients" in need of healing or employment (Mirza, 2005, p. 271). This may add to the debate of whether engagement with digital media can widen or reduce the long-standing class-based academic–vocational divide in education.

Although North America has a long history in teaching media production to youth for the purpose of job-readiness (Goldfarb, 2002; Goodman, 2005; Poyntz & Hoechsmann, 2011), the popularity of Florida's creative class argument indicates that we are entering an era in which such practices are being reconfigured: creativity is commodified, learning outcomes are capital-driven, and young people are portrayed as potential skilled workers for global competitiveness. For example, youth programs are understood in terms of practicing vocational skills and are often evaluated by the numbers of youth employed, even though this is just one of many purposes. With the growing public discourse linking economics and education, community workers have to organize their programs' recruitment, fund-raising, activities, and assessment through a justification that links youth media arts practices to the productivity in the market. Likewise, the demographic definition of youth is purposefully marketed as a group of creative future workers who can "successfully compete individually (and as a creative collective) in capitalizing

DOI: 10.1057/9781137475176.0006

opportunities created by changing technologies" (Gude, 2013, p. 38). As Bragg and Buckingham (2014) argue, in the context of today's proliferation of digital media, the construct of youth is "a site of struggle over its social meanings, a repository of hopes and fears for the future of the world in times of socioeconomic, technological and cultural change" (pp. 273–274).

However, with the changing economy, despite the growing recognition of a need to prepare 21st-century learners as creative workers for an innovative labor market, there is a lack of evidence showing how young people develop employment potential and career interests related to digital- and art-making (Campbell, 2013; Hoechsmann & Low, 2008; Sefton-Green & Brown, 2014). As media educator Brian Goldfarb (2002) asks, "Will media across the curriculum be the cutting edge of progressive pedagogy, or the newest vo-tech track for a class of worker?" (p. 71). This question remains crucial as educators are at a junction of today's employment trends in the creative industries and youths' learning experiences with emerging technologies. Furthermore, there is little research that shows how community-based youth media programs operate under the impact of an economic rationale for learning, as well as how professionals working with youth navigate and negotiate their practices under the influence of a neoliberal view of education. This deficiency indicates that, in the discourse of linking creativity to economic advancement for individuals and society, we have caught up with its promise, yet overlooked its predicament. Therefore, understanding these politics in economics and education allows educators and community workers to be critical about the impact of societal changes on youth digital participation and art-making in informal learning settings.

The Frames Film Project

Since neoliberal economics and politics continue to shape education, I examine how they affect the changing landscape of digital-mediated learning in informal educational environments. I do this through a close examination of how one community-based youth media arts program operates and how its youth participants' learning experiences take shape. In particular, I discuss how the neoliberal economic rationalization is realized and justified by community professionals to strategically navigate their program delivery and public outreach. The discussion is based

DOI: 10.1057/9781137475176.0006

on a program of field observation, interviews, visual documentation, and analysis of learning processes and artistic products.

The Frames Film Project (Frames) is a Vancouver-based film production and life skills program provided at no cost to youth aged 16–28 with mental health and/or substance abuse issues. It provides opportunities for youth to learn the basics of film production, create their own short films, and gain life skills. The program structure includes film production workshops and mentorship, as well as a film screening and community dialogue event at the end of each intake. Frames is initiated by Frog Hollow Neighbourhood House (FHNH), a nonprofit organization providing programs and services that meet the needs of community members. As FHNH is located in one of the most culturally diverse areas in the oldest part of the City of Vancouver, youth participants of Frames come from different ethnic and social status backgrounds, including immigrant, Aboriginal, and ethnic and social minority groups. They are referred to the program by professionals, such as counselors, social workers, or teachers. Each program intake takes about four months to complete. Participants meet once a week on Thursday evenings for three hours and on several weekends for shooting and editing, with refreshments and transit tickets provided for each meeting. The program coordinator and assistants are professional filmmakers; they work closely with FHNH youth services staff and an advisory board regarding curriculum design, youth consultation, and program logistics.

Institutional support

The idea of initiating a film program for the youth services division at FHNH began with the director's vision of using arts-based programming to connect the individual inhabitants with the life of the neighborhood. When seeking program funding, many community program coordinators today search for a balance between the fulfillment of their multifaceted organizational goals and the requirement to frame their programs through a lens of workplace skills training, in order to meet the objectives of the funding agencies (Bunyan, 2012). To secure funds for Frames, indeed, FHNH staff have to work together to address this challenge, with the result that Frames "is very employment focused," as described by Jennie, the program facilitator of youth services. While Frames is promoted as a skills training program servicing a specific group of youth in need of jobs and experiences, FHNH's vision of empowering

DOI: 10.1057/9781137475176.0006

youth through an arts-based approach to film production has been manifested in various forms throughout the program. Acknowledging this complexity, FHNH administrators like Gary and Jennie provide considerable support to Kryshan, the program coordinator, who takes charge in shaping the direction of Frames. Kryshan appreciates the administrative staff's role as mentors and advisors in providing higher level oversight of administrating. As Kryshan states it, "they also give me a lot of creative freedom to run things however I want" (Kryshan, personal communication, April 2013). Kryshan reflects on the freedom that allows the program to unfold organically:

> I have creative freedom from my employers, and then I give a certain amount of freedom to the youth, which allows the program to evolve as it goes along. There's no fixed way to run the program, and it's sort of based on the youth and their comfort level, skill level, interest level and various factors. (Kryshan, personal communication, April 2013)

At the same time, the staff members work closely to ensure that grant objectives are met and that issues like pedagogical beliefs, community engagement and student needs are underlined. As Jennie expresses, "*Frames* is a lot more integrated than we had initially thought it might be" (Jennie, personal communication, March 2013). Together they have developed a consensus that youth media programming is socially constructed and locally situated. By recognizing the social nature of learning, they assert that filmmaking is a means for individuals to articulate their understanding of and relationship to the world, as well as to react to the ways that audiovisual experience can inform social actions.

Pedagogical approach

Kryshan, the program coordinator, is the key player at Frames. He is a professional filmmaker with 13 years experience in directing short films and producing corporate videos and news segments. Kryshan is also a film educator and youth mentor for several community-based youth film programs locally and internationally. Having a professional filmmaker like Kryshan on board was unexpected for FHNH. As Jennie says,

> We didn't think that we would find the program coordinator that we have. We didn't think we would find someone on his level of knowledge regarding film production. What we wanted was a unique set of skills—you have to be a youth worker who also happens to be a filmmaker. And we thought we would find someone who's stronger on the youth worker side with a little

> bit of filmmaking skills, but we found somebody who is just such a perfect combination. (Jennie, personal communication, March 2013)

As a result, Kryshan has played an important role in reorienting Frames' program approach from a traditional model of skills development workshop to one of cultivating youth potential through hands-on experiences and relationship building. Jennie described this shift: "Originally we thought the program focus would be on workshops on life skills, but what youths are doing is they're learning about communication through making a film as a group, which is fantastic" (Jennie, personal communication, March 2013).

Kryshan's approach to media education does not prioritize skill training or therapeutic outcomes but is about learning in relation to film. Understanding film as a compelling way of storytelling, Kryshan views film production as offering young people forms of engagement that relate to issues such as agency, empowerment, and self-esteem. Commenting on his teaching philosophy, Kryshan says,

> Sometimes I would think of a few different breaks from the filmmaking process, but mostly I incorporate everything, because to me the film, the process of making film encompasses all those things—life skills, job skills, voice or techniques. (Kryshan, personal communication, April 2013)

Frames' educational approach utilizes film as a vehicle for storytelling; it is "a methodology for participatory content creation" (Burgess & Klaebe, 2009, p. 50). For many Frames youth who have a history of living with or recovering from personal challenges, storytelling becomes an entry point for them to articulate their own personal narratives through scriptwriting, acting, directing, set design, special effects makeup, and editing. They are encouraged to process, share, and cathartically express their interpretations of life, hope, and fear that enact them "into a way of knowing that privileges direct experience" (Fletcher & Cambre, 2009, p. 117). Natalie, a program assistant who has a background in scriptwriting, comments on how Frames youth learned to communicate personal stories with a collective vision of film production in mind:

> My main contribution would be in helping them take their stories from their head to the page. Also helping them to develop a creative vision of script, so they understand a script isn't just making sense to themselves. I mean, a script needs to make sense to every single person who is going to read it afterwards...Of course there're challenges along the way. We are working with

DOI: 10.1057/9781137475176.0006

> youth that have had issues in the past, mental health issues and such. So they may get more stressed out. I mean it's the start—when you have deadlines, we have to get scripted on time, you have to be on set, and you have to be present. It could be harder for people who are doubting themselves, having insecurity. It's a challenge I guess to not only teach them from the standpoint of knowing their past histories and helping in any way that we can, but also to hold them accountable as adult. It is important to hold them to the standard of being a reliable member of the team, and also making sure that the decisions we make benefit all the students as a whole. (Natalie, personal communication, April 2013)

At Frames, storytelling through film is a process that traverses between overcoming personal challenges and learning to be team players in order to meet production deadlines and ensure quality. Such a creative endeavor moves beyond the personal pleasure of digital-making and is not about "merely playing around with the latest technological gadgets" (Buckingham, 2007, p. 98). Instead, it creates and fosters a culture of professionalism in which youth are expected to act professionally like those working in the film industry. Kryshan and Natalie, who work as filmmakers during the day and teach at Frames in the evening, treat Frames youth like professional colleagues, referring to examples from film sets and using film production language for communication. While Frames youths are amateurs learning how to produce their first short films, acting professionally then becomes a strategy, as well as an attitude, that encourages them to work with others, resolve conflicts, and develop relationships in order to hold each other accountable.

After each intake, Frames youth host a film screening event that includes a community dialogue segment in a professional theater. They show their films and also engage with the audience for question and answer (Q&A) sessions. By doing this in one of the most well-known theaters in Vancouver, youth experience being professional filmmakers and that their stories have been heard. As Poyntz and Hoechsmann (2011) argue, "Creative practices place youth in conversation with others and thus offer opportunities for young people to address the sedimented social discourses and cultural practices that shape their experiences" (p. 307). Over the past two years, hundreds of community members have attended these events. They appreciate that the event is youth-focused and provide a unique space to engage and dialogue with youth.

DOI: 10.1057/9781137475176.0006

Discussion

From multidisciplinary collaboration to pedagogical possibilities

Behind *Frames* is a team of professionals who work collaboratively to make the program function. With support from its director, FHNH's youth service division administrates the program and provides resources for Kryshan to run Frames. The advisory board of Frames performs a vital role in youth service and consultation, since the program works with young people with special needs and challenges. Board members include mental health professionals, youth workers and consultants, a program evaluator, and community organization leaders. Additionally, several filmmakers in local film industries and media educators in other community-based youth media programs also act as consultants for employment referral and program delivery. For example, as Jennie puts it,

> When an issue came up with the youth in the program, and there have been a number of them, we reached out to one of the professionals on our advisory committee, maybe a drug and alcohol councilor, saying, "This youth is experiencing this, how can we help him?" Or reaching out to other community support like if someone is having housing concerns—so really using the youth network we have that's up there. (Jennie, personal communication, March 2013)

This youth network that Jennie describes reflects an ecological perspective for youth media programming that features a network of practitioners across disciplines in supporting youth learning. FHNH can be viewed as an ecosystem that sustains the network between its members (administrators, educators, community worker, and participants), who work together toward the shared goal of developing youth potential through digital technologies.

Frames' model offers a response to the interdisciplinary nature of youthhood in the age of digital culture situated in the current economic climate. That is, to cope with increasingly overlapping responsibilities, multidisciplinary professionals are working together to navigate the complex interplay between external societal expectations dominated by an economic rationality and internal learning dynamics that span issues ranging from instructors' pedagogical beliefs to learners' personal challenges. Internally, Frames' staff work collectively to understand each other's roles in terms of program development and

DOI: 10.1057/9781137475176.0006

execution. Externally, each of them deals with a variety of audiences to meet different agendas, needs, and expectations. For example, the administrator is responsible for bridging the conversation between the funders' visions and how the program is delivered; the program facilitator oversees the public outreach strategies for community members; and the program coordinator communicates with the advisory board regarding the therapeutic aspect of youth learning progress, as well as working with youth through the process of filmmaking. In short, since professionals conceptualize Frames from their disparate areas of expertise, this example shows a model of youth programming that consists of a high degree of trust, respect, coordination, communication, and negotiation in order to meet various aims and objectives. This model highlights a set of cooperative efforts in institutional, pedagogical, and organizational aspects, and suggests that successful community initiatives are strongly tied to a collective commitment and intersected social networks among all members. Further, as the impact of neoliberalism is undeniably part of the contemporary cultural landscape, Frames suggests a new model of social practice: specifically ways of youth program delivery that underline collaboration and dialogue, and span disciplines including social work, community development, and the arts.

Career aspiration meets youth empowerment

While Frames is not exclusively a media program that emphasizes skills-based training careers in the film industry, youth are drawn to this profession because of Kryshan's active professional connection to the film industry in Vancouver, one of the major film production cities in North America. On one occasion, Kryshan connected Frames youth with some professionals through Crazy8s, a Vancouver-based filmmaking challenge that supports six groups of emerging filmmakers to produce six short films in eight days.[3] Kryshan explains his intent:

> I think it's important for [Frame youth] to see how the industry works, but in a way that it is a good first impression through visiting a set or helping out with something that they feel comfortable. Even it's just being a helper or an assistant, a lower position in a hierarchy. When they do that, they not only see how the industry really works but also do it in a way that they feel supported. So yeah, Crazy8s was a good fit that way. (Kryshan, personal communication, April 2013)

DOI: 10.1057/9781137475176.0006

Kryshan sees the intensity and timeframe of Crazy8s as offering a unique chance for Frames youth to have a glance at how the film industry operates. He explains,

> This wasn't like a normal experience of how you start out in the film industry where you would get advice much later, maybe several months later. But in this case there was support and advice right away with the set up of Crazy8s. One of youths visited all the sets and a few of them helped out on some sets but they weren't given too much tasks too soon. I tried to put them in touch with people in the industry that are friends of mine and would treat them well and maybe give them little bits of advice here and there. So they were either getting advice from my friends in the industry or on the sets they visited. (Kryshan, personal communication, April 2013)

Mainly, Frames youth were offered an opportunity to shadow the behind-the-scenes film crew of Crazy8s. Reflecting on her experience of touring six film sets in two days, Cat, an 18-year-old Frames participant, describes:

> Sunday I showed up at a yoga studio where "In the Deep" was filming. I knew they were short of production assistants. Luckily, Hayden, a co-producer had recognized me from the shoot before and agreed to take me on. Throughout the day, I carried a heavy suitcase down the stairs, helped a truck back off into the street so it wouldn't hit any bikers or pedestrians, guarded the crew's belongings, went up 8 flights of stairs to bring towels... I was shown how to set up and take apart C-stands by the key grip. At their next location near English Bay, Erik the producer came by and asked if I wanted to go to the next set. So I hopped on board. The final set was at Guys and Dolls, a billiards place at Main St. and Broadway St. I met the DIT (digital imaging technician), the director, a publicist, the editor, and the 3rd AD (assistant director). The pull focus guy was eager to explain how the pull focus worked. I had known from before that when a camera moved, it would be out of focus as the depths of fields changed. Now I know what pull focus is. (Cat, personal communication, April 2013)

Learning opportunities like Crazy8s provide an alternative dimension that enriches youth experience at Frames. As Kryshan describes Crazy8s: "this experience is more of a mentorship, rather than an apprenticeship" (Kryshan, personal communication, April 2013). Frames youths were invited to experience an in-between role of apprentice and student as a unique learning experience. They gained exposure to the industry through a carefully prearranged conduit provided by Kryshan while learning to navigate their lives and make their first film. Such an

DOI: 10.1057/9781137475176.0006

experience has turned out to be "the focal point of the production process" (Goldfarb, 2002, p. 72) providing youths with therapeutic inspiration, such as for self-motivation and self-esteem. For some of the Frames youths who have constantly experienced multilayered barriers in life, they feel inspired by having the chance to shadow a professional film crew, to be held accountable on film sets, and to be treated like professional adults. This experience has become the basis that allows youth to envision their potential in overcoming personal and social barriers while constructing a sense of belonging endorsed by peer-to-peer learning, adult mentorship, and institutional support. Because of this exposure, Frames youth become motivated to work collaboratively and respectfully in order to push themselves for higher production standards as the final screening event takes place. Alongside, Kryshan's commitment to high production quality has inspired the youth to believe in themselves and perform their best. Kryshan's high expectation for film quality has to do with his strong advocacy for youth voice, and not so much with skill development or vocational training. This involves encouraging them to enter film contests in order to enable youths' new media productions to have a better chance to be seen by wider audiences. As a result, youths' high-quality media products have emerged as marketing by-products used for program promotion by administrators. Following this, an employment opportunity came unexpectedly in 2014, as two nonprofit organizations commissioned a group of Frames youth to produce public service announcement videos.

Creativity reconsidered

The idea of job-readiness for future creative workers has become a marketing strategy for youth media programs like Frames, especially in the City of Vancouver where support for creative economy is rapidly mounting as new film and digital media firms set their sights to settle or expand (Brinton, 2012). Moreover, with the concern of economic uncertainty, Frames may be seen as the right fit for fostering marginalized youth's creativity under a neoliberal agenda for education, which is

> About equipping people with the skills they need to live full lives; the ability to respond creatively and confidently to changing situation and unfamiliar demands, to solve the problems and challenges they face at home, in education, at work, to make a positive contribution to the life of their communities. (Bentley & Selzer, 1999, p. 9)

DOI: 10.1057/9781137475176.0006

Such assumptions seem reasonable as the logic of "neoliberalism has become integral to common-sense understandings among the populace at large" (Harvey, 2005, p. 39). However, underlying such traits is the market-driven focus on youths' final products of creative performances and artifacts associated with the discourse of neoliberal productivity. Despite that, how such generic traits are actually demonstrated through Frames is unclear. In fact, the lack of conversation around what it means to be creative individuals in Frames' program delivery and youth participation suggests two things. First, it signals a disconnect between the impact of youth creative practices on young people's everyday lives and the type of values that public discourses and cultural policies recognize. Second, it points to a much-needed conversation among professionals in the sectors of creative industries, cultural policies, community development, and education on ways of fostering creativity in the 21st century, an understanding not only driven by the need of a changing economy but also recognizing the multicontextual nature of creativity where economic, social, cultural, and pedagogical considerations intersect. Therefore, as educators, we must recall that being creative is more than a simple set of procedures leading to particular end results and, more importantly, individuals' acts of expression and communication cannot be reduced to the commodity value of their creative endeavor. While harnessing creativity to economic growth signals an end from which individuals and the society may benefit, the experience of learning to be creative may become detached from its rich human context and disconnected from both self and world. As art educator Gude (2013) contends, when creativity is linked to demanded productivity, it is a "stripped down concept of creativity, a creative capacity unsullied by the messiness of artistic insight, cultural complexity, human need, or ethical considerations" (p. 38).

With current economic arguments well positioned to shape education locally and globally, perceiving creativity as a social construct is more important than ever. Such a discourse has a long history in academia (Anderson & Milbrandt, 2005; Buckingham & Willett, 2009; Freedman, 2007; Gablik, 1991; Gee, 2004; Sefton-Green & Sinker, 2000). For cultural theorist Raymond Williams (1983), creativity is seen as a human capacity rather than a source of economic value. More recently, media theorist David Gauntlett (2011) argues, "Creativity is a gift, not in the sense of it being a talent, but in the sense that it is a way of sharing meaningful things, ideas, or wisdom, which form bridges between

DOI: 10.1057/9781137475176.0006

people and communities" (p. 245). In the case of youths' participation at Frames in digital media, creativity can be understood as a social practice that allows young people to navigate imaginatively through personal challenges and the world in which they live. Thus, creativity becomes a means not only of personal development but also of social inclusion. Particularly in relation to the latter it is thereby meaningful not merely for the pursuit of profit or career. Rather, it is the creative realization of how meaning can be constructed through a collective endeavor of digital- and art-making, as well as how youth creative practices can be seen as an avenue of intervention to facilitate and promote dialogue between community members and youth on the margins. In line with this thinking, according to Goldfarb (2002), the genre of film is "the medium" to nurture "self-analysis and interpersonal relationship building, enhancing reflective insights into dynamics of a group and its distinct identity" (p. 115). Considering the role of media production from an educational standpoint, Frames' conceptualization of youth creative products and artworks is less about representing the commodification of creativity, and more about encouraging young people to perceive media products "as moments in a process of meaning production" (Goldfarb, 2002, p. 75). Such moments, including young people's brief exposure to the local film industry and their collective efforts in organizing the screening event, suggest an ongoing state that allows mediations on learning to take place and enables the crossing of boundaries between personal and social responsibilities. Such moments also inform us about how young people's creative learning with digital media is imbued with social relations as manifested through "an active relationship with others and modes of information" (Sefton-Green, 2011, p. 250). In the context of contemporary digital-mediated culture, creativity is thus seen as evolving, fluid, and intertwined, embedded in lived experience, and organized around real-world situations and simulations.

Conclusion

Today the neoliberal argument of creativity for successful societies is mounting because of economic uncertainty across the globe. While this ensures that the societal values regarding creative endeavors are a spotlight of attention in public and educational discourse, we as educators, however, must recognize the multidimensional qualities of creativity

DOI: 10.1057/9781137475176.0006

and how its complexity goes beyond a simple formula for economic growth. With the advancement of digital technologies linked closely to the discourse about creativity and the economics, this chapter shows that community program administrators have learned to utilize the economic justification to support their programming. While the economic rationale is not clearly exemplified in their internal program implementation, it is strategically embraced as a marketing tool to guide the organization's relationships with funders and the public. By presenting a unique case description and discussion of Frames Film Project hosted by FHNH, I intend to provide perspectives on ways of understanding, conceptualizing, and interpreting what it means to be creative learners in the 21st century. I argue that creativity is more than a generic measurement of individual competence or political slogans driven by economic needs. Instead, it exhibits a form of social experience that "is not simply a matter of spontaneous 'self-expression' but something that occurs within—and indeed depends upon—particular social contexts and cultural conventions" (Buckingham, 2009, p. 235). Further, it also suggests a need to recognize the complexity of learning in the 21st century in which *how* young people learn to make digital media artworks is as important as *what* they make, that is, a perspective that looks into how youth-made media and youth progression of making intersect. This connection allows us to envision ways of learning that enact and sustain the empowerment of youth voices, and facilitate personal growth and development, trusting learning relationships, career aspiration, cultural collaboration, and exchange among adult professionals and young people.

Notes

1 For more in-depth discussion on the changing conceptions of creativity in relation to art education see Zimmerman (2009) and Costantino (2011). Additionally, Buckingham (2009) offers a comprehensive characterization of the role of creativity in digital art-making, whereas Harris (2014) articulates the relationships among creativity, aesthetics, and imagination in the 21st century.

2 Social theorist David Harvey (2005) defined neoliberalism as "a theory of political economic practices that proposes that human well-being can be best advanced by liberating individual entrepreneurial freedom, characterized by strong private property rights, free markets and free trade. The role of the state is to create and preserve an institutional framework appropriate to such activities" (p. 2). I recognize the discourse of neoliberalism as a complex

DOI: 10.1057/9781137475176.0006

argument; my deployment of the term here is to reveal how current discourses around young people's learning with digital media, whether explicit or not, are under the impact of neoliberalism. More discussion of neoliberalism and education can be seen in Harvey (2010) and Hill and Kumanl (2009).

3 More information about Crazy8s see http://www.crazy8s.cc

References

Anderson, T. & Milbrandt, M. (2005). *Art for Life*. New York, NY: McGraw-Hill.

Bentley, T. & Selzer, K. (1999). *The Creative Age: Knowledge and Skills for the New Economy*. London: Demos.

Bragg, S. & Buckingham, D. (2014). Conclusion: elusive "youth." In D. Buckingham, S. Bragg, & M. J. Kehily (Eds), *Youth Culture in the Age of Global Media* (pp. 272–287). New York, NY: Palgrave Macmillan.

Brinton, S. (2012). *From the Margins to the Mainstream: Moving BC's Creative Industries Forward*. Suebee Media Consulting. http://books.bc.ca/wp-content/uploads/2012/04/CI_Report_Web_Final.pdf.

Buckingham, D. (2007). *Beyond Technology: Children's Learning in the Age of Digital Culture*. Cambridge, England: Polity Press.

Buckingham, D. (2009). Power to the people? The past and future of amateur video. In D. Buckingham & R. Willett (Eds), *Video Cultures: Media Technology and Everyday Creativity* (pp. 230–238). New York, NY: Palgrave Macmillan.

Buckingham, D. & Willett, R. (2009). (Eds). *Video Cultures: Media Technology and Everyday Creativity*. New York, NY: Palgrave Macmillan.

Bunyan, P. (2012). Partnership, the big society and community organizing: between romanticizing, problematizing and politicizing community. *Community Development Journal*, 47(2), 1–15.

Burgess, J. & Klaebe, H. (2009). Using digital storytelling to capture responses to the apology. *3CMedia: Journal of Community, Citizen's and Third Sector Media and Communication*, (5), 44–61.

Campbell, M. (2013). *Out of the Basement: Youth Cultural Production in Practice and in Policy*. Montreal, QC: McGill-Queen's University Press.

Caves, R. (2000). *Creative Industries: Contracts between Art and Commerce*. Cambridge, MA: Harvard University Press.

DOI: 10.1057/9781137475176.0006

Chan, J. & Thomas, K. (2013). Introduction to the chapters. In K. Thomas & J. Chan (Eds), *Handbook of Research on Creativity* (pp. 1–20). Northampton, MA: Edward Elgar Publishing.

Costantino, T. (2011). Contemporary aesthetic theory and models of creativity in visual arts education in the United States. In J. Sefton-Green, P. Thomson, K. Jones, & L. Bresler (Eds), *The Routledge International Handbook of Creative Learning* (pp. 159–167). New York, NY: Routledge.

Couldry, N. (2010). *Why Voice Matters: Culture and Politics after Neoliberalism*. Thousand Oaks, CA: Sage Publications Ltd.

Craft, A. (2011). *Creativity and Education Futures: Learning in a Digital Age*. Sterling, VA: Trentham Books.

Darras, B. (2011). Creativity, creative class, smart power, social reproduction and symbolic violence. In J. Sefton-Green, P. Thomson, K. Jones, & L. Bresler (Eds), *The Routledge International Handbook of Creative Learning* (pp. 90–98). New York, NY: Routledge.

Drotner, K. (2011). The cult of creativity: opposition, incorporation, transformation. In J. Sefton-Green, P. Thomson, K. Jones, & L. Bresler (Eds), *The Routledge International Handbook of Creative Learning* (pp. 72–80). New York, NY: Routledge.

Fisherkeller, J. (2013). Young people producing media. In D. Lemish (Ed.), *The Routledge International Handbook of Children, Adolescents, and Media* (pp. 344–350). New York, NY: Routledge.

Fisherkeller, J. (2011). Introduction. In J. Fisherkeller (Ed.) *International Perspectives on Youth Media: Cultures of Production and Education* (pp. 1–21). New York, NY: Peter Lang.

Fletcher, C. & Cambre, C. (2009). Digital storytelling and implicated scholarship in the classroom. *Journal of Canadian Studies, 43*(1), 109–130.

Florida, R. (2002). *The Rise of the Creative Class: And How It's Transforming Work, Leisure and Everyday Life*. New York, NY: Basic Books.

Freedman, K. (2007). Artmaking/troubling: creativity, policy, and leadership in art education. *Studies in Art Education, 48*(2), 204–217.

Gablik, S. (1991). *The Reenchantment of Art*. New York, NY: Thames and Hudson.

Gauntlett, D. (2011). *Making Is Connecting: The Social Meaning of Creativity from DIY and Knitting to YouTube and Web 2.0*. Malden, MA: Polity Press.

Gee, J. P. (2004). *Situated Learning and Literacy: A Critique of Traditional Schooling*. London: Routledge.

DOI: 10.1057/9781137475176.0006

Giroux, H. (2011). Neoliberal politics as failed sociality: youth and the crisis of higher education. *Logos: A Journal of Modern Society & Culture, 10*(2). Retrieved from http://logosjournal.com/2011/neoliberal-politics-as-failed-sociality-youth-and-the-crisis-of-higher-education/.

Goldfarb, B. (2002). *Visual Pedagogy: Media Cultures in and beyond the Classroom*. Durham, NC: Duke University Press.

Goodman, S. (2005). The practice and principles of teaching critical literacy at the educational video center. In G. Schwarz & P. Brown (Eds), *Media Literacy: Transforming Curriculum and Teaching* (pp. 206–228). Malden, MA: National Society for the Study of Education.

Gude, O. (2013). Questioning creativity. In N. Addison & L. Burgress (Eds), *Debates in Art and Design Education* (pp. 37–42). New York, NY: Routledge.

Harris, A. (2014). *The Creative Turn: Toward a New Aesthetic Imaginary*. Rotterdam, the Netherlands: Sense Publishers.

Harvey, D (2005). *A Brief History of Neoliberalism*. New York, NY: Oxford University Press.

Harvey, D. (2010). *The Enigma of Capital and the Crises of Capitalism*. London, England: Profile Books.

Hesmondhalgh, D. (2007). *The Cultural Industries*. London, UK: Sage.

Hill, D. & Kumanl, R. (2009). *Global Neoliberalism and Education and Its Consequences*. New York, NY: Routledge.

Hoechsmann, M. & Low, B. (2008). *Reading Youth Writing: New Literacies, Cultural Studies and Education*. New York, NY: Peter Lang.

Hull, G. & Nelson, M. (2010). Literacy, media, and morality: making the case for an aesthetic turn. In M. Prinsloo & M. Baynham (Eds), *The Future of Literacy Studies* (pp. 199–220). Houndmills, England: Palgrave Macmillan.

Jagodzinski, J. (2013). The hijacking of creativity: the dilemma of contemporary art education. In N. Addison & L. Burgess (Eds), *Debates in Art and Design Education* (pp. 23–34). New York, NY: Routledge.

Jenkins, H. (2008). *Convergence Culture: Where Old and New Media Collide*. New York, NY: New York University Press.

Jones, K. (2011). Capitalism, creativity and learning: some chapters in a relationship. In J. Sefton-Green, P. Thomson, K. Jones, & L. Bresler (Eds), *The Routledge International Handbook of Creative Learning* (pp. 15–26). New York, NY: Routledge.

DOI: 10.1057/9781137475176.0006

Jones, R. (Ed.). (2012). *Discourse and Creativity*. New York, NY: Routledge.

Lacy, S. (2010). *Leaving Art: Writings on Performance, Politics, and Publics, 1974–2007*. Durham, NC: Duke University Press.

Lin, C. & Bruce, B. (2013). Engaging youth in underserved communities through digital-mediated art learning experiences for community inquiry. *Studies in Art Education*, 54(4), 335–348.

Mirza, M. (2005). The therapeutic state. *International Journal of Cultural Policy*, *11*(3), 261–273.

Osborne, T. (2003). Against "creativity": a philistine rant. *Economy and Society*, *32*(4), 707–525.

Peppler, K. & Solomou, M. (2011). Building creativity: collaborative learning and creativity in social media environments. *On the Horizon*, *19*(1), pp. 13–23.

Poyntz, S. (2009). "On behalf of a shared world": Arendtian politics in a culture of youth media production. *Review of Education, Pedagogy and Cultural Studies*, *31*(4), 365–386.

Poyntz, S. & Hoechsmann, M. (2011). Not just philosophizing: producing effective youth media and communication projects. In J. Fisherkeller (Ed.), *International Perspectives on Youth Media: Cultures of Production and Education* (pp. 301–316). New York, NY: Peter Lang Publishing.

Rogers, J. (2013). Dewey's liberalisms: depression-era insights for the Great Recession. *International Studies in Sociology of Education*, *23*(3), pp. 204–223.

Sefton-Green, J. (2011). Creative digital cultures: informal learning beyond the school. In J. Sefton-Green, P. Thomson, K. Jones, & L. Bresler (Eds), *The Routledge International Handbook of Creative Learning* (pp. 244–252). New York, NY: Routledge.

Sefton-Green, J. & Brown, L. (2014). *Mapping Learner Progression into Digital Creativity: Catalysts & Disconnects*. Nominet Trust. Retrieved from http://www.nominettrust.org.uk/knowledge-centre/articles/mapping-learner-progression-digital-creativity.

Sefton-Green, J. & Sinker, R. (2000). *Evaluating Creativity: Making and Learning by Young People*. New York, NY: Routledge.

Sope, E. (2006). Beyond literacy and voice in youth media education. *McGill Journal of Education*, *41*(3), 197–213.

Throsby, D. (2001). *Economics and Culture*. Cambridge, UK: Cambridge University Press.

DOI: 10.1057/9781137475176.0006

Williams, R. (1983). *Key Words: A Vocabulary of Culture and Society* (2nd edn.). London: Fontana.

Zimmerman, E. (2009). Reconceptualizing the role of creativity in art education theory and practice. *Studies in Art Education*, 50(4), 382–399.

DOI: 10.1057/9781137475176.0006

3

Amplifying Youth Cultural Practices by Engaging and Developing Professional Identity through Social Media

Martin Lalonde and Juan Carlos Castro

Abstract: *This chapter presents an analysis of the pedagogical and curricular methods used at the La Relève program at Maison Kekpart, a new media arts community program in Montreal, Quebec, established to support students (13-to 17-years-olds) who are at risk of dropping out of school. We specifically examine how social media is deployed to create a space that fosters positive and professional relationships between the artists-educators, youth, and the cultural environments. Our analysis demonstrated that the implementation of social media in an educational setting promoted ownership of the cultural objects produced by youth and further fostered engagement in their social and academic communities.*

Keywords: aesthetic engagement; at-risk youth; digital visual culture; peer-learning; social media

Black, Joanna, Juan Carlos Castro, and Ching-Chiu Lin. *Youth Practices in Digital Arts and New Media: Learning in Formal and Informal Settings.* New York: Palgrave Macmillan, 2015. DOI: 10.1057/9781137475176.0007.

 DOI: 10.1057/9781137475176.0007

Educational concerns in Quebec

Over the last 20 years, policy makers in Quebec have sought to address the high dropout rate in secondary schools. The early 1990s marked a period where the nature of curricular activities in the Quebec general academic program was out of step with the social and cultural reality of students. At that time, the Quebec Ministry of Education consulted educators and the general population to develop a better sense of the situation and began to strategize solutions (Gouvernement du Québec, 1996). It was emphasized in the reports published after these consultations that the Quebec education system should be renewed to equip young people to meet the challenges of an information and technology-based society and economy (Gouvernement du Québec, 1997; Ministère de l'Éducation, du Loisir et du Sport du Québec, 1997). As a result, new reforms were implemented across the province in the early 2000s to restructure educational programs in order to promote the success of all students and to further embed learning in real-world situations to meet the diverse learning styles of each individual. Also, new to the reforms was the inclusion of culture as a foundational and critical feature incorporated into every educational program. Each local school board was given more freedom in determining the content and educational methods to promote civic education and the empowerment of its students (Guimont, 2009; Lessard & Portelance, 2002).

Along with these changes digital technologies evolved rapidly in cultural and educational practices. At the beginning of Quebec's educational reforms the Internet was still unavailable to most schools, and now, almost 20 years later, the majority of young people have powerful mobile computing devices connected to the Internet. These changes in the digital media landscape also contributed to significant changes in the theoretical foundations and educational methods used in schools across the province. Policy makers recognized this influx of new technology; however, today there still is little effective integration in most pedagogical and curricular models in the province.

Emerging digital youth cultural practices now stand in contrast to policies and procedures in Quebec school culture. Young students are divided between two distinct worlds. On the one hand, their social life unfolds in a variety of physical and virtual spaces, which overlap each other. They are actively involved in identity construction and performance in online (Castro, 2014), cultural practices, and civic participation

DOI: 10.1057/9781137475176.0007

with and through digital media. On the other hand, their academic proficiency develops in an environment where their personal, cultural, and social practices are not fully recognized. In school environments, the use of mobile computing, digital cameras, and autonomous Internet is often prohibited. In young people's everyday lives, they are used to having a physical and virtual presence whereas in school only the physical is permitted. Ironically, this is the same educational challenge the reforms sought to address.

The gap between youth cultural practices outside of school and inside of school is a fertile ground for thinking about how to engage learners, especially those who are more likely to drop out of school. What can educational institutions learn from young people's interactions in the virtual communities? How have young people developed new knowledge and social and cultural practices in these contexts? What motivates young people to engage in online and off-line communities and how does the cohesion of such communities function? Reflection on these questions yields strategies to enable educators to meet the demands of contemporary society while creating a natural and sustained interest on the part of young people.

In this chapter, we present our research of Maison Kekpart (www.kekpart.com), a community-based new media arts center that serves youth aged 13–17 years who are at risk of dropping out of school. The curriculum at Maison Kekpart is designed to provide the experience of a professional internship in new media arts while pursuing students' creative interests. Within Maison Kekpart, there is also an array of services to support the social, academic, and personal dimensions of the students involved. Young people are attracted to programs like Maison Kekpart because they seek professional competencies that apply outside of school.

Social media use in the classroom is a polarizing topic for educators and administrators. Some school districts and community centers embrace these technologies fully while others restrict and/or ban their use altogether (Lajoie, Légaré, Grouzet, Malo, Marcotte, & Campos, 2006). What education centers like Maison Kekpart offer to new media arts teaching are strategies for using social media responsibly and professionally. Their approach offers innovative methods for integrating these technologies into informal and formal educational contexts.

DOI: 10.1057/9781137475176.0007

The Quebec context

Dropouts

The graduation rates from secondary school today exhibit that the current situation is much better than 20 years ago; however, the dropout problem is now concentrated among specific demographic groups. Youth from less affluent neighborhoods are more at risk of dropping out of school. Educational services provided are less abundant and usually of lower quality than those enjoyed by youth from affluent backgrounds. The contrast is evident when one looks at the socioeconomic map of the island of Montreal; the western part consists of relatively affluent neighborhoods and has a dropout rate under 15 percent while the east portion of the island consists of less affluent neighborhoods with a dropout rate above 20–25 percent (Duchaine, 2013). Maison Kekpart is located in Longueuil, which is outside of Montreal's east end, where the school board reported a general school dropout rate of 19.7 percent in 2010, and the percentage for the boys is at 23.7 percent (Ministère de l'Éducation, du Loisir et du Sport du Québec, 2012). Even though school board funding is equalized through the provincial government, there is a strong link between the economic conditions students come from and educational engagement in Quebec.

At-risk youth

In Montreal and surrounding areas, youth who are most at risk are those who live in socioeconomic disparity. In Longueuil, high schools are struggling to meet the varied needs of at-risk students. It is difficult for these young people to have access to the individualized services they need to be successful in school. Often, a student who is classified as at-risk is transitioned to secondary school auxiliary programs where they are left to themselves because the host institution is not able to meet their individualized needs. Quebec researchers Chouinard, Bowen, Cartier, Desbiens, Laurier, & Plante (2005) and Marcotte (2012; Marcotte, Fortin, & Cloutier, 2012) reported that the individualization of curriculum was a prerequisite for at-risk student success.

DOI: 10.1057/9781137475176.0007

Governmental strategies: regular and special programs for at-risk youth

Since the implementation of the Quebec educational reform, schools are required to develop vocational training that is representative of the culture of their community. In many instances, sports and arts are common vocational subject areas. These strategies are aimed at fostering a strong school culture in which young people can connect with their education. Such programs aim to provide students with opportunities to create connections between their school activities and their daily life outside of school. There are programs such as "La culture, toute une école!" (Ministère de l'Éducation, du Loisir et du Sport, n.d.a) and "I Care About School" (Gouvernement du Québec & Ministère de l'Éducation, du Loisir et du Sport, 2009). Such programs are the result of giving more autonomy to educational stakeholders in the development of their school's curriculum. Over the past 14 years, local training programs have emerged and flourished throughout the province.

Complementing in-school programs are educational initiatives outside of the formal schooling structure. Maison Kekpart, which belongs to a network of community centers, is one example. Schools in the city of Longueuil rely on Maison Kekpart, which offers a range of services to meet the needs of at-risk students. Many times youth in the formal school system who are not engaged with regular academic courses are transitioned into classes that are mandated to help them transfer out of school before graduation to earn a work experience certification. Essentially these classes function as holding areas that are constituted of youths with behavioral issues and learning difficulties or are at risk of dropping out. With dwindling resources, schools have little to offer these students. School administrators are now considering informal programs such as Maison Kekpart to meet the needs of their at-risk student populations. Commenting on how these programs are a chance for young people to receive the necessary support and opportunity to participate in a meaningful educational environment, Jean Perron, a former school administrator of one of the main secondary schools in Longueuil, stated,

> For at risk youth, the program fostered the talents of young people that were not recognized and cultivated at school. By the same occasion, it leads to significant achievements for these students who are often accustomed to failure in school.

DOI: 10.1057/9781137475176.0007

He also stated that the specific contribution of community centers, like Maison Kekpart, to the academic success of adolescents is that

> There is the individual monitoring and the long term support of the student that the school and the workplace are not able to offer. This is what makes a difference. This is the unique contribution of community centers. (M. Perron, personal communication, May 24, 2013)

Academic motivation

According to Lieury and Fenouillet (1997) one of the conditions that contribute to a student dropping out is a perceived lack of control in school. When an at-risk student does not feel like they have a choice in the curriculum they can feel disconnected. Oftentimes, the student then acts out, disengages, or willfully resists authority. As a result, the student is disciplined, which just compounds the repeated failures they have experienced trying to engage with their education. Over time, school becomes synonymous with social exclusion and powerlessness for at-risk youth.

Research on academic motivation in Quebec has demonstrated that educational interventions that rely on external rewards are mostly unsuccessful (Chouinard et al., 2005). To succeed in keeping at-risk students from dropping out, educational interventions need to cultivate intrinsic motivation (Viau, 2005). Youth who have the opportunity to make considered choices demonstrate a sense of self-worth and satisfaction (Arnett, 2000, 2007; Côté, 2002, 2005; Marcotte et al., 2012). Cultivating and supporting self-determination in learning is a fundamental quality in the development of educational programming for at-risk youth. These youth need opportunities for experimentation and expression where they can have positive experiences and identify topics that will sustain their interest.

Tourrilhes (2008) emphasized the importance of giving educational freedom to young people so that they can begin the process of identity construction, which will determine the professional, civic, and social competencies that will guide them through their adult life. Marcotte's (Marcotte et al., 2012) research also recognized the need for positive identity construction and performance. According to her, it is necessary to promote a sense of ownership in the learner so that they can determine educational outcomes that connect with their everyday lives. These findings point to a key condition for engaging at-risk youths with their education, which is learning connected to their real-world needs.

DOI: 10.1057/9781137475176.0007

Chouinard et al. (2005), drawing on the research of Rubin, Bukowski, and Parker (1998), stress the importance for students to feel comfortable in the school environment. He highlights the responsibility of educators to create the conditions for a healthy social environment. When students do not have the support of their peers and teacher in learning they will be less likely to have positive experiences in school (Ollendick, 1992). These findings illustrate the responsibility the educator plays as a mediator of social relationships to foster positive interactions between individuals within a learning community. Having students play a role in determining the subject of inquiry, coupled with being situated in positive social relationships with peers, greatly increases student engagement and retention. Educational engagement is directly related to the type and quality of social relationships experienced by adolescents (Chouinard et al., 2005).

Maison Kekpart

Maison Kekpart is a community center directly linked to at-risk students' formal schooling. Situated within Maison Kekpart is La Relève program, which is considered by the school board as preemployment training. It is presented as an internship option to students who come from classes connected to employment programs within the region's secondary schools. Academic advisors and teachers from schools are not involved in the La Relève program. It is a self-contained program that is designed by administrators and educators from Maison Kekpart. Program courses are therefore not formally assessed and do not result in grades on the students' transcripts. The goal is to provide a professional work experience for young people facing academic challenges. At the end of their training in La Relève, they receive a work experience certification recognizing their participation in an internship in one of the areas of multimedia production. The main challenge for the La Relève program administrators is that their training program competes with other school board partners that offer students experiences as grocery or retail store clerks, janitor's assistants, or factory worker. These partners often welcome interns for a paid work placement that requires no secondary education.

On the South Shore of Montreal, there are many socioeconomic challenges. The city of Longueuil has an urban mosaic of neighborhoods

DOI: 10.1057/9781137475176.0007

where affluent homes mix with social housing for low-income individuals and families. According to the Department of Public Health, the poverty rate is higher than the provincial average, and there are a multitude of social challenges (Dallaire & Agence de la santé et des services sociaux de la Montérégie, Québec, 2011). Maison Kekpart was founded in the neighborhood of St. Pius X in the early 1980s to serve youth who faced socioeconomic challenges threatening their well-being and education. Today, its primary mission is to provide youth with a variety of educational and social programs to address personal, family, social, and educational issues.

What distinguishes Maison Kekpart from other community centers in the province is the abundance and variety of educational services that are offered. At the foundation, there is a team of social workers specializing in various fields whose mandate is to host and mentor young people who come to the center voluntarily. On their premises are game rooms, a community kitchen, social room, and the offices of administrators at the center. It is the other wings of the center that reflect the current expansion of the youth center's mission. On the main floor there is an auditorium and an exhibition hall. In the basement are digital arts production labs and classrooms. These facilities are similar to a visual and performing arts center as they can present theatrical and musical events while also hosting a digital arts training and exhibition center. The stakeholders at Maison Kekpart have structured a goal-oriented environment that emphasizes digital artistic creation in the service of educational and social integration of at-risk youth.

At Maison Kekpart, students have access to the latest technology in the fields of digital imaging, video production, and sound design. The students work with professionals in the community by participating in various programs led by the instructors. Students at Maison Kekpart are supported by professional technical staff who have experience in industry new media production. These resources enable students to have educational experiences closely linked to professional practice.

La Relève

Our research focused on one of Maison Kekpart's programs devoted to using digital media production to engage 13- to 17-year-old at-risk youths. The La Relève educational program is a work placement where

DOI: 10.1057/9781137475176.0007

young people are encouraged to develop professional skills in one of three multimedia disciplines. They can choose from course offerings in sound design, digital imaging, and video production. By enrolling in the program, they retain their regular school schedule during the first three days of the week and in the remainder report to Maison Kekpart for their internship. Their attendance at school during the year is a prerequisite for their participation in La Relève. Each of the three classes is constituted of six students for the duration of one 18-week semester. Councilors at La Relève propose a schedule where students can take two different courses within a school year.

According to Annick Monger, the head administrator of the program, La Relève is supported by a diversity of funding sources including various contributions from public and private sources. Private sector contributions come from two local financial institutions that support youth service development on an annual basis. Funding provided by these companies is granted through internal programs aimed at addressing particular issues encountered by the local population. Next are the funds administered by a foundation (Fondation Québec Jeunes, n.d.) whose mission is to support "projects and resources that help young people aged 11–17 years in their transition to adulthood." Various private companies are the basis of this foundation, and each of them contributes through specific development objectives.

Federal and provincial funding supports the program on an ongoing basis, enabling multiple levels of services within the Kekpart community center. Funds from the Industry Canada Ministry (Industry Canada, n.d.) that have been granted to the program through a nonprofit organization (Carrefour Internet Montérégien, n.d.) are designed to "assist its clientele in the use of information and communications technology and to initiate and develop innovative projects, implement new services and adopt new management and communication practices."

Finally, at the provincial level, the Ministère de l'Éducation, du Loisir et du Sport supports La Relève through a program designed to enable community initiatives in fields traditionally reserved for the education sector. The objectives of this program are "aimed at creating a favorable environment for the development of Community action in the Quebec community and to publicize, promote and support community action organizations whose primary mission is similar to the educational mission of the Department and their combination" (Ministère de l'Éducation, du Loisir et du Sport du Québec, n.d.b).

DOI: 10.1057/9781137475176.0007

Students

The directors of Maison Kekpart designed the La Relève educational program in order to meet the needs of secondary schools in Longueuil. These schools sought learning environments that could accommodate at-risk students through educational programs that keep them in the school system while preparing their transition to the workplace. For example, adjacent to the Maison Kekpart, Jacques-Rousseau High School is a secondary school with over 2100 students. It is home to many classes and groups of students with difficulties and particular needs. These classes are made up, on average, of 12–15 students who have failed to meet the standards of secondary school graduation and would rather attend vocational training. However, there are few professional options available to these students because most training programs require a secondary school diploma. The program is presented to students in their regular schools as an option for their professional internship. Students have to apply to be selected for the La Relève program.

Program objectives

The La Relève program first seeks to engage students with their attitudes toward learning to reduce school dropout rates. The educators seek to create a space of experimentation and expression for students with the goal that it will contribute to their academic motivation. Second, the program is designed to foster the social reintegration of youth. Students who enroll in programs like La Relève have suffered from social marginalization by having been placed in special classes outside from the regular academic system. Having been removed from regular student status within their school community seriously hampers their educational and social integration. These young people must learn to be part of a community in which they express themselves, engage, and develop their interests. Third, the program seeks to contribute to the construction of a substantial body of knowledge and competencies in the field of new media production. The program does not seek to only train multimedia technicians; rather they are also deeply invested in developing students' professional identities and the know-how of youth through the development of digital literacies.

Educational methods

The objectives of the program are designed to meet the needs of students who have differing learning challenges. The main objective is to restore

DOI: 10.1057/9781137475176.0007

or establish a positive attitude to the social experience of schooling. Leaders of the program also seek to promote the intrinsic motivation of their participants and create a space where students can positively focus on identity construction as professionals. The teachers of La Relève understand that it is critical to rebuild a social bond between these young people and the institution of school. Students are reacquainted to the institutional environment through positive learning experiences. The La Relève program emphasizes the dissemination of their creative digital practice through social media. It is through the production of varied digital content that participants collectively engage with each other in building individual and collective social identity(ies) and meaningful cultural practices. The educators of La Relève in conjunction with digital media professionals aim to build positive relationships between at-risk youth and educational institutions. From our research we have identified that the process of establishing a self-representation through cultural reappropriation using digital and social media practices represents a key strategy of the educators to reconnect at-risk youths with their schooling.

Method

Combining ethnographic observation (Creswell, 1998; Denzin, 2003) with image-based research methods (Grauer, Irwin, Cosson, & Wilson, 2001; Grauer, Irwin, & Zimmerman, 2003; Leavy, 2009; Weber & Mitchell, 2004), we examined the organizational and educational structures of Maison Kekpart, the La Relève program, teacher pedagogy and curricula, and students' social and digital practices. The ethnographic approach described here is a process of generating meaning through a critical examination of cultural content by social actors that are, as a result of decisions made by individuals within different structures, constituting these environments. According to Goodley, Lawthom, Clough, and Moore (2004), "ethnography is a viable way to make sense of informal learning environments and learning culture" (p. 56). Our use of ethnographic methods focuses on the relationships observed within the formal educational site of Maison Kekpart that allow us to identify the social dynamics connected to the learning and teaching that occur in these environments.

As researchers, we followed the youth at Maison Kekpart as they progressed in their learning throughout one semester. Informal sharing

DOI: 10.1057/9781137475176.0007

occurred through conversations and through semi-structured formal interviews with both students and teachers. These interviews formed a significant part of the research data. We collected multiple forms of data (e.g., field notes, a series of interview transcripts, observations of teaching activities and developments, photos and video material of these observations, copies of visual artifacts of the young participants, and teaching materials from the teachers). We organized and analyzed the collected data according to various themes established in the initial thematic coding of the data.

Our data analysis was consistent with the theories of Wolcott (1994), offering an interpretative model in three steps: description, analysis, and interpretation of the cultural group. The first two steps sought to identify recurring thematic motifs while the third step sought to draw inferences from descriptions and analysis in order to construct an interpretation of the cultural group. These preliminary results from the descriptive and analytical data, as well as the semantic interpretation, were triangulated from different sources with visual artifacts of cultural groups: media production participants, educators, and the program.

We sought to develop an integrated understanding based on the specific media practices at La Relève and as such also deployed image-based research methods. We used photographic elicitation (Harper, 2002), a process whereby photo and video documentation encouraged participants to reflect critically on their learning and knowledge creation (Grauer, 2000; Grauer et al., 2001; Sinner, Leggo, Irwin, Gouzouasis, & Grauer, 2006; Mitchell, Weber, & Pithouse, 2009).

Findings

Teaching

The first thing that distinguishes the educational practices at Maison Kekpart is the academic and professional profile of the educators. The teachers do not have traditional training and certification. Instead, they are young artists working in their respective fields. For example, the teacher of the sound design workshop is an established artist who has enjoyed success and visibility on a number of major television stations in Quebec. The other two teachers have similar profiles. These three educators share the belief that teaching is mostly a way for them to finance

DOI: 10.1057/9781137475176.0007

their creative and professional goals, which represents a unique career path compared to regular school teachers. Their primary purpose for teaching is to provide support for their artistic practice. However, we have found that such educators draw a number of unique pedagogical approaches from their professional practice which they apply toward transforming youth cultural practices into curricular activities, thus fostering connections between students and their schooling.

What distinguishes the skills of these teachers is their knowledge and practice of self-promotion through social media. In two cases, the teachers have multiple accounts on popular social media platforms. These accounts are used for social networking and dissemination of their artistic practice. We have observed that the social spaces of these teachers tended to overlap. That is to say that the personal accounts of the artist educators were used to publish and share professional content while also socializing with others. When questioned on the subject, they argued that the goal remained the same, namely to gain the most visibility possible. What is relevant here is that they also used their personal and professional social media accounts to connect with the students they taught at Maison Kekpart. They leveraged their digital identities to create a practice of professionalism beyond the physical structures of school.

Responses from interviews with three educators and the program director of Maison Kekpart clearly support the notion that digital media arts are an effective way to support at-risk students in their process of social and academic reintegration. Successful completion of the La Relève program leads to certification that students can use in the completion of their formal schooling. However, the teachers are also concerned with creating a social atmosphere that is welcoming without the constraints of formal schooling that students are used to experiencing. It is in this context that educators have developed strategies that enable them to integrate into the community of youth they serve, while integrating young people into their professional community. Social media is used heavily to accomplish this integration.

Deploying social media to build relationships

Educational centers such as Maison Kekpart enjoy a wide latitude in the use of social media when compared to schools. The teachers determine the way in which they use social media to fulfill their mission to engage at-risk youth. They use social media to present and promote

DOI: 10.1057/9781137475176.0007

the activities of their classes and the program in general. The creation, management, and curation of digital identities through social media are a critical part of their pedagogy. The social environment of young people offers an important space for the deployment and distribution of content generated by youth at Maison Kekpart as well as in their personal social network. There is a hybridity of spaces provided by social media in which the different social and cultural environments that are traveled by an individual converge. The educators at Maison Kekpart believe that being present and active in these spaces promotes a more holistic and comprehensive approach to engaging youth. This activity is part of belonging to society: one in which youths can manifest their identity through professional practice by participating in a coconstruction process of cultural knowledge.

Next we briefly describe the pedagogical practices of the educators to illustrate this approach at Maison Kekpart. First, Maison Kekpart has a number of official social media accounts across varied platforms. The coordinators carefully select platforms where their students are active. Facebook and YouTube are two popular social media platforms for youth at Maison Kekpart. Coordinators and instructors of the La Relève program keep these accounts up-to-date by posting the productions they have done with their classes while linking the account to personal profiles of students who attended the program. The educators' and administrators' intention is to promote positive interactions between members of the community in order to check the program's accounts on a daily basis and to respond to student and community profiles. These responses and interactions may be a comment made to a student on her or his Facebook wall, the publication of any media reporting activities, or simply mentioning appreciation of published content by students. The educators' and coordinators' objective is to create links within the community so that positive and professional interactions arise independently around content created by the La Relève program. It is important to highlight that the institutional social media accounts of the Maison Kekpart connect with the personal accounts of their students.

Similarly, teachers in the La Relève program use their own professional social media accounts to connect to their students' accounts. The emphasis on connecting with students online is not limited to promoting the content and interactions of the La Relève program but also modeling professional behavior online. It is via this link that young people have access to the content and interactions with their instructors

DOI: 10.1057/9781137475176.0007

beyond the classroom. In essence, it connects at-risk youth to another social world that provides new potentials for what it means to be and become a professional artist. This has become a hybrid social environment in the sense that many people, from many differing contexts and from different backgrounds, flow through the networks formed by the teachers of Maison Kekpart. These practices are consistent with the precepts outlined above where teachers are the primary mediators of social interaction. Their role is to create fertile spaces and moments of interaction where young people can engage through practice and the lines of inquiry that they have identified and chosen. Students benefit from these informal channels of communication as different social realities interface. We also note that teachers have a window looking into the sociocultural world in which their students live in a way that they can assess their students' interests and cultural productions to incorporate them into the curriculum of their respective courses at La Relève.

Cultural practices of youth in the curriculum

Teachers at Maison Kekpart attach great importance to cultural practices of youth. They determine the learning objectives of the curriculum through the practices of youth. We observed that the students at Maison Kekpart who displayed a strong interest toward a particular digital practice ended up influencing the directions undertaken in group projects. In the case of a student sharing and publishing content through social media, the teacher often invites them to present and explain how this creative production is of interest to herself or himself. Students are encouraged to think about the meaning of their cultural practices and the differing elements that relate to their practice. Often youth and educators debate the different types of digital cultural productions as a source for developing the curricular directions of the course. We observed certain recurring types of digital production coming from digital youth culture incorporated into the La Relève curriculum. They are as follows:

- The "Selfie" or Self-Portrait: this is any form of self-representation of an individual subject through digital imagery.
- Mash-up: a visual and/or audio production involving several elements on the same topic and from different sources that are combined into a static or time-based composition.
- Remake: a conceptual or formal reinterpretation of an existing production from the repertoire of popular digital culture. It can use

DOI: 10.1057/9781137475176.0007

one or more elements of differing nature that refer to the original production. These elements can be sampled from the original content of the work or they can also be just conceptual references to the original. Unlike a mash-up, the remake reformulates specific aspects of a particular production rather than referring to a series of different sources and works. It augments or diverts certain characteristics or the totality of the original production.

- Parody: this is a humorous reinterpretation of an existing work. This type of production takes different forms, such as a mash-up, to the original production where the authors refer to a humorous reference of the original production.
- Internet Meme: the meme is often referred to as a viral media production where a particular idea or production style is often adopted online. This phenomenon leads regularly to reinterpretations of this trend by users such as the Harlem Shake, or Planking.

These different types of digital and online cultural productions represent the types of curricular projects in the La Relève program. The curricular designs draw direct inspiration from digital youth culture. They were observed by teachers and presented by the students themselves to be discussed and analyzed in the classroom. We observed that the teachers demonstrated a more traditional approach in their artistic practice. For example, the teacher artists do not use digital media from the Internet to use for works like mash-ups, parodies, or remakes in their own practice.

The construction of public presence online

We have observed the emergence of creative digital media production and dissemination to public online spaces resonated as an essential feature of being a professional. Students, as well as educators, are always attentive to the concept of audience when designing and producing media. The most common types of productions that we observed (parody, mash-up, documentary fandom, recovery, self-portrait, fiction, or comment) all carried a strong self-representational dimension for the participating teens.

The students reflected that they wanted to learn the professional technical skills; however, they also perceived digital production as part of a precise and contextualized social process. New media production is strongly linked to social media dissemination that is conducive for the

DOI: 10.1057/9781137475176.0007

personal representation of self by the students. New media production for these students is contextualized; it is an integral part of broad and various social perspectives, such as function and necessity. The social reasoning and motivation behind projects are seriously considered as integral steps in the creative process.

This is consistent with danah boyd's (2014) research, which emphasizes that teens are continually considering a target audience when representing themselves online. Often, teens are targeting the social groups of those they know off-line. For teens, the use of social media is mainly to maintain relationships originating from off-line contexts (boyd, 2014). When youths publish content online, it often acts as a kind of intervention within their social group in which they negotiate their identity construction.

Here, Bourriaud's (1999) aesthetics of everyday life is particularly applicable: to create anything, is to create yourself. Young people are aware of the social significance of their virtual presence and seek to create statements about themselves that will fit a specific context for a specific audience. The youth we interviewed are keenly aware of the permanence of what they post online. This is one reason that they want to master professional production techniques that enable them to carefully control their self-representation online.

Learning to craft beautiful things

Beauty, or the well-crafted image, was a topic that was present in most of our interviews with students. It is a dominant concern that is apparent through all of the activities taking place in the program. Learning objectives designed and implemented by the educators reflect these concerns. As we have described earlier, production generated by the students is driven by the cultural forms that they encounter and use in their digital cultural environments. Youth's construct of being beautiful often refers to the standard of productions inherent to the music and film industry of popular culture.

Youth want to learn how professionals make seductive images and content; they want to work with professional equipment to create beautiful images. Their notions regarding beauty often referred to popular visual culture, such as major Hollywood films, in which they observe a level of technical mastery. Attainment of beautiful images was not an end in and of itself, but was seen as the vehicle of their personal message.

DOI: 10.1057/9781137475176.0007

For students, their message has impact when it is well crafted. Beautiful means well crafted, and well crafted means that a high mastery of technique and standards of production has been achieved. What teens want to do is provoke a reaction in their off-line and virtual communities with striking new media content. The media object becomes an extension and expression of self. Online publishing emulates communication within their social group as teens are always considering the look of their production to their targeted audience.

Our findings take into account that the teachers' main objective remains the socialization of dropouts into a healthy relationship within the institution of schooling. For them, the goal is to teach students to be part of a group and interact, dually, with their own interests and for the good of the community. As we noted earlier, teachers are mediators of social relationships, creating the conditions to promote positive interactions. In this case, the common goals and interests act as a catalyst for group inquiry, learning, and knowledge creations.

Instant production

Social media thrives on instant production and dissemination of content. This stands in stark contrast to the current regulatory policies found in many schools, which seeks to control communication throughout the school. We found that at Maison Kekpart the effective use of social media in the classroom was punctual and synchronized with the daily activities of classes. In this case, social media is not exclusively used to publish finished projects. Rather, it is utilized to share the artistic process that students and teachers participate in together. Educators and students published their developing media practices on a daily basis seeking an extension of the dialogues that occurred in the real world.

Teachers at Maison Kekpart told us in interviews that the use of social media is beneficial for the effectiveness and richness of learning in their classrooms. Posting and commenting requires careful attention on media sites in order to maintain a sustained presence within these networks. If a day or more passes without publishing or interaction it can often diminish the motivation and interactions, resulting in students leaving the established networks to pursue other social media networks. Educators and policy makers are present in the virtual environments of young people in the same way as they are in their off-line educational environment.

DOI: 10.1057/9781137475176.0007

Teaching in the off- and online worlds of teens

Finally, we observe an obvious difference of perspective when considering the definitions of academic engagement and comparing it with the sense of commitment enacted by the teachers and students in the La Relève program at Maison Kekpart. That is, school engagement is not a keen interest in class work or test scores. Rather, engagement for the students and teachers participated in our study means the coconstruction of knowledge; a sense of belonging to a community of shared interest; the sharing of positive messages through media productions; recognition and encouragement of peers; media literacy as a language and as a form of social engagement; as well as the ability to participate in a peer learning group. The main distinction between these students' school environment and Maison Kekpart is that engagement in schools is often measured through external disciplinary actions and motivations, while in Maison Kekpart engagement is defined as the intrinsic motivation of the learner in a larger community of learning. Such findings are consistent with theories of collaborative learning (Chan, 2013; Johnson, Johnson, & Holubec, 1994; Kafai & Fields, 2013) motivated where the learning and teaching of the participants was enacted in a shared creative community. In this chapter, the use of social media is indicative of holistic approaches to education wherein there emerges a mutual exchange of engagement, not only in the subject but in the performance of a practice of professionalism that these youth craved.

References

Arnett, J. J. (2000). Emerging adulthood: a theory of development from the late teens through the twenties. *American Psychologist, 55*(5), 469–480. doi:10.1037/0003-066X.55.5.469.

Arnett, J. J. (2007). Suffering, selfish, slackers? Myths and reality about emerging adults. *Journal of Youth and Adolescence, 36*(1), 23–29.

Bourriaud, N. (1999). *Formes de vie l'art moderne et l'invention de soi.* Paris: Denoël.

boyd, d. (2014). *It's Complicated: The Social Lives of Networked Teens.* London: Yale University Press.

Carrefour Internet Montérégien. (n.d.). Carrefour Internet (CARIM). Retrieved from http://www.carim.ca/index.html.

DOI: 10.1057/9781137475176.0007

Castro, J. C. (2014). Constructing, performing, and perceiving identity(ies) in the place of online art education. *The Journal of Culture Research in Art Education, 31*(1), 31–53.

Chan, C. K. K. (2013). Collaborative knowledge building: towards a knowledge creation perspective. In C. E. Hmelo-Silver, C. A. Chinn, C. K. K. Chan, & A. M. O'Donnell (Eds), *The International Handbook of Collaborative Learning* (pp. 437–461). New York, NY: Routledge, Taylor & Francis Group.

Chouinard, R., Bowen, F., Cartier, S. C., Desbiens, N., Laurier, M., & Plante, I. (2005). L'effet de différentes approches évaluatives sur l'engagement et la persévérance scolaires dans le contexte du passage du primaire au secondaire. Retrieved from http://www.frqsc.gouv.qc.ca/upload/editeur/RF-Chouinard(1).pdf.

Côté, J. E. (2002). The role of identity capital in the transition to adulthood: the individualization thesis examined. *Journal of Youth Studies, 5*(2), 117–134. doi:10.1080/13676260220134403.

Côté, J. E. (2005). Identity capital, social capital and the wider benefits of learning: generating resources facilitative of social cohesion. *London Review of Education, 3*(3), 221–237. doi:10.1080/14748460500372382.

Creswell, J. (1998). *Qualitative Inquiry and Research Design*. Thousand Oaks, CA: Sage Publications.

Dallaire, L. & Agence de la santé et des services sociaux de la Montérégie, Québec. (2011). Pauvreté et exclusion sociale: Forum régional pour la solidarité et l'inclusion sociale, Agglomération de Longueuil. Retrieved from http://www.cdclongueuil.org/client_file/ upload/document/Presentation%20DSP%20au20Forum27oct2011.pdf

Denzin, N. (2003). Performing [auto]ethnography politically. *The Review of Education, Pedagogy, and Cultural Studies, 25*(3), 257–278.

Duchaine, G. (2013, December 12). *Décrochage scolaire: une île, deux mondes*. Retrieved from http://www.lapresse.ca/actualites/education/201312/11/01-4720160-decrochage-scolaire- une-ile-deux-mondes.php.

Fondation Québec Jeunes. (n.d.). Fondation Québec Jeunes. Retrieved from http://www.fondationquebecjeunes.com/.

Goodley, D., Lawthom, R., Clough, P., & Moore, M. (2004). *Researching Life Stories: Method, Theory and Analyses in a Biographical Age*. London: Routledge Falmer.

DOI: 10.1057/9781137475176.0007

Gouvernement du Québec. (1996). *Les états généraux sur l'éducation 1995–1996. Exposé de la situation*. Document accessible à l'adresse: http://www.uquebec.ca

Gouvernement du Québec. (1997). *Prendre le virage du succès*. Rapport du groupe de travail sur la réforme du curriculum. Québec: Ministère de l'Éducation.

Gouvernement du Québec & Ministère de l'Éducation, du Loisir et du Sport. (2009). *I Care about School! All Together for Student Success*. Ministère de l'éducation, du loisir et du sport. Retrieved from http://collections.banq.qc.ca/ark:/52327/1946436

Grauer, K. (2000). The art of teaching art teachers. *Australian Art Education Journal*, 22(2), 19–24.

Grauer, K. (2001). Images for understanding: Snapshots of learning through the arts. International Journal of Education & the Arts, 2(9). Retrieved from http://www.ijea.org/v2n9/index.html.

Grauer, K., Irwin, R., & Zimmerman, E. (2003). Introduction. In K. Grauer, R. Irwin, & E. Zimmerman. (Eds), *Women Art Educators V: Conversations across Time; Remembering, Revisioning, and Reconsidering* (pp. 3–4). Vancouver, BC: Canadian Society for Education through Art and the National Art Education Association.

Guimont, G. (2009). La réforme de l'éducation et le renouveau pédagogique au Québec: les faits saillants. *Pédagogie Collégiale, 22*(3), 29–34.

Harper, D. (2002). Talking about pictures: a case for photo elicitation. *Visual Studies, 17*(1), 13–26.

Industry Canada. (n.d.). Minister of Industry—Industry Canada. Retrieved from http://www.ic.gc.ca/eic/site/icgc.nsf/eng/h_07019.html

Johnson, D. W., Johnson, R. T., & Holubec, E. J. (1994). *Cooperative Learning in the Classroom*. Alexandria, VA: Association for Supervision and Curriculum Development.

Kafai, Y. B. & Fields, D. A. (2013). Collaboration in informal learning environments: access and participation in youth virtual communities. In C. E. Hmelo-Silver, C. A. Chinn, C. K. K. Chan, & A. M. O'Donnell (Eds), *The International Handbook of Collaborative Learning* (pp. 437–461). New York, NY: Routledge, Taylor & Francis Group.

Lajoie, J., Légaré, C., Grouzet, F., Malo, C., Marcotte, D., & Campos, M. (2006). *Academos à l'école: Intégration d'un programme de cybermentorat vocationnel aux activités d'orientation au deuxième cycle du secondaire.*

DOI: 10.1057/9781137475176.0007

Retrieved from http://www.frqsc.gouv.qc.ca/upload/editeur/actionConcerte/RF-JacquesLajoie.pdf

Leavy, P. (2009). *Method Meets Art: Arts-Based Research Practice*. New York, NY: Guildford Press.

Lessard, C. & Portelance, L. (2002). *Réflexions sur la réforme curriculaire au Québec*. Québec: Centrale des syndicats du Québec.

Lieury, A. & Fenouillet, F. (1997). *Motivation et réussite scolaire*. Paris: Dunod.

Marcotte, J. (2012). Breaking down the forgotten half: exploratory profiles of youths in Quebec's adult education centers. *Educational Researcher, 41*(6), 191–200.

Marcotte, J., Fortin, L., & Cloutier, R. (2012). *Portrait personnel, familial et scolaire des jeunes adultes émergents (16–24 ans) accédant aux secteurs adultes du secondaire : identification des facteurs associés à la persévérance et à l'abandon au sein de ces milieux scolaires*. Retrieved from http://www.fqrsc.gouv.qc.ca/upload/capsules_recherche/fichiers/capsule_35.pdf.

Ministère de l'Éducation, du Loisir et du Sport. (n.d. a). La culture, toute une école! Retrieved October 24, 2014, from http://www.mels.gouv.qc.ca/contenus-communs/education/culture-education/.

Ministère de l'Éducation, du Loisir et du Sport du Québec. (n.d. b). Programme d'action communautaire sur le terrain de l'éducation (PACTE). Retrieved October 28, 2014, from http://www.mels.gouv.qc.ca/organismes-communautaires/organismes-communautaires/programme-daction-communautaire-pacte/

Ministère de l'Éducation, du Loisir et du Sport du Québec. (2012). *Taux de sorties sans diplôme ni qualification (décrochage annuel), parmi les sortants, en formation générale des jeunes, selon le sexe, par réseau d'enseignement et par commission scolaire, 2010–2011*.

Ministère de l'Éducation du Québec. (1997). *L'école, tout un programme: énoncé de politique éducative*. Gouvernement du Québec, Ministère de l'Éducation.

Mitchell, C., Weber, S., & Pithouse, K. (2009). Facing the public: using photography for self-study and social action. In D. Tidwell, M. Heston, & L. Fitzgerald (Eds), *Research Methods for the Self-Study of Practice* (pp. 119–134). New York, NY: Springer.

Ollendick, T. H. (1992). Sociometric status and academic, behavioral, and psychological adjustment: a five-year longitudinal study. *Journal of Councilling and Clinical Psychology, 60*(1), 80–87.

DOI: 10.1057/9781137475176.0007

Rubin, K. H., Bukowski, W., & Parker, G. (1998). Peer interactions, relationships, and groups. In W. Damon & N. Eisenberg (Eds), *Handbook of Child Psychology, Vol. 3: Social, Emotional and Personality Development* (pp. 619–700). New York, NY: John Wiley.

Sinner, A., Leggo, C., Irwin, R., Gouzouasis, P., & Grauer, K. (2006). Arts-based educational research dissertations: reviewing the practices of new scholars. *Canadian Journal of Education, 29*(4), 1223–1270.

Tourrilhes, C. (2008). *Construction sociale d'une jeunesse en difficulté: innovations et ruptures.* Paris: L'Harmattan.

Viau, R. (2005). *La motivation en contexte scolaire.* Bruxelles: De Boeck université.

Weber, S. & Mitchell, C. (2004). Using visual and artistic modes of representation for self-study. In J. Loughran, M. Hamilton, V. LaBoskey, & T. Russell (Eds), *International Handbook of self study of Teaching and Teacher Education Practices* (pp. 979–1037). Dordrecht: Kluwer Press.

Wolcott, H. F. (1994). *Transforming Qualitative Data: Description, Analysis, and Interpretation.* Thousand Oaks, CA: Sage Publications.

DOI: 10.1057/9781137475176.0007

4

New Media Pedagogy in Two High Schools: A Look at Formal Learning Environments

Joanna Black

Abstract: *In this chapter the author discusses a comparative case study undertaken during 2010–2012 at two very different Canadian secondary schools located in the prairies. Two educators are examined and both are notable for their outstanding practices in teaching digital technologies: specifically addressed are lived experiences of two art teachers involved in designing, implementing, and running their own new media programs. A specific focus is on innovative curricula development and flexible, creative, pedagogical practice situated in the formal learning sector or environment. In this chapter there is a specific center of attention placed upon educators' narratives, their teaching circumstances, and dynamics shaping their particular lived situations. Through examination of these model programs, I will discuss best practices of two teachers who have met with success.*

Keywords: animation; art education; communities of practice; creative learning; digital technologies; film; formal learning; in-school learning; new media; schools; teenagers

Black, Joanna, Juan Carlos Castro, and Ching-Chiu Lin. *Youth Practices in Digital Arts and New Media: Learning in Formal and Informal Settings.* New York: Palgrave Macmillan, 2015. DOI: 10.1057/9781137475176.0008.

Case study of new media pedagogy in two high schools: a look at formal learning environments

For this chapter the research was undertaken in Manitoba, a central province located within the Canadian prairies. Until 2008, Manitoba's school arts curricula had been separate within the public schools, dividing visual arts curricula from that of drama, music, and dance (Manitoba Education and Training, 1988, 1990, 1993).

The Manitoba K-8 visual arts curricula lack written explanations to aid educators in the area of contemporary art or new media. In the high school curricula, however, it is briefly stated that current approaches in art production should be taught (2014, p. 8), and a further brief statement indicates that art educators should address contemporary technologies in current professional art practice (Manitoba Education, 2014, pp. 16, 26). What is truly lacking are rich, detailed theoretical, practical, historical, or contextual descriptions in which the authors address the methodology of writing curricula and incorporating digital technologies in Manitoba's art classrooms.

What is currently happening in Manitoba public schools? The overriding theoretical approach is to provide a democratic education for all children with core values of equity and social justice "to ensure that all members of the school community enjoy access to the same rights and privileges" (Weisshaar, 2012, p. 1). This stance results in Manitoba lacking what many other provinces in Canada have: namely, specialized arts programming for the talented and gifted as well as art magnet schools (Morin, 2010). Even though new curricula are emerging in Manitoba, it has been found (Morin, 2010) that teachers are currently not integrating the arts and are focusing more on the individual art areas of dance, drama, visual arts, and music.

Use of digital technologies overall is sporadic and employed on an ad hoc basis. Currently, most of the digital technologies are found in music classrooms across this province (Morin, 2010). Moreover, Morin has found that there is a dearth of technological equipment and digital teaching facilities in visual art, dance, and drama. She writes, "there is a lack of technology-based arts pedagogy reported by some schools, particularly in the areas of new media and the use of specialized technology for particular art forms" (2010, p. 118). Moreover, it is evident that there is a gap between the digital world of the students outside of school and the nondigital world of the arts programs within formal settings as

DOI: 10.1057/9781137475176.0008

a result of the dominate use of technology by our youths (Jenkins, 2009) versus the shortage of new media programs within Manitoba schools. Surprisingly, despite this dim situation, there are a few successful models of new media integration within arts programs as a result of supportive administrators and keen, dedicated, skilled, and knowledgeable teachers who see the value of new media in their formal school settings and therefore have pushed to establish their digital programs.

In this chapter I present my research concerning two Manitoba secondary schools' new media programs. Two educators are examined and both are notable for their outstanding practices in teaching digital technologies: specifically addressed are the lived experiences of these two art teachers involved in designing, implementing, and running their own new media programs. The two high schools selected are Applewood Alternative High School and Orangeville Collegiate Institute (pseudonyms are used for schools and teachers). The art educators within these programs are some of the few teachers, who, within Manitoba, were early to embrace digital technologies in the arts (Mr. Smith, personal communication, October 3, 2011).

Research methodology

Within a two-year period, case study research was conducted in two middle schools and two high schools[1] and it is framed within comparative case study research (Denzin & Lincoln, 2000) in order to analyze commonalities and differences between teachers' stories and factors shaping their particular life situations. However, owing to their highly specialized and extremely well-developed programs, only the high schools are examined.[2] The focus of this paper is on the schools' two art educators and Heads of the Department who have overseen these digital programs from their beginnings. This method highlights, as Shulman (2007) states, the practical situations, practices, actions, and visions of practitioners to help us imagine and shape curricula and programs that meet future needs, which in the case of this research relates to educational new media practices. To this end, I examined two new media educators' approaches to pedagogy, their teaching situations, and their personal perspectives concerning their school programs.

The two high schools selected, Applewood Alternative High School and Orangeville Collegiate Institute, were easy to select as they stood out from

DOI: 10.1057/9781137475176.0008

the other schools in regard to their program excellence.[3] Typical of case study research, multiple methods of data collection were used (Merriam, 1998; Stake, 1994; Yin, 2003). These included: (1) qualitative, semi-structured videotaped interviews (Merriam, 1998) and open-ended teacher interviews (Yin, 2003) which were audio recorded, videotaped, and transcribed and returned for "member checks" (Stake, 1995, p. 115). Concurrent with the research, an ongoing (2) collection of videotapes and photographs of student work was undertaken in order to provide contextual understandings pertaining to the curricula and final new media productions. Additionally, (3) photography and texts of archival data were gathered for purposes of "document review" (Stake, 1995) which included newsletters, school profiles, digital software and hardware information as well as media information. As well, (4) participant observation of classrooms was conducted throughout the two academic years pertaining to pedagogy and teacher–student relationships. Finally, (5) field notes were written about the classroom observations. To ensure confidentiality, pseudonyms were used for all the schools, educators, and students involved in the research.

Further, data were examined using a successive iterative process to uncover "correspondence and patterns" (Stake, 1995; Yin, 2003), which helped strengthen internal validity. Patterns were examined regarding personal, social, and cultural categories (Stake, 1995) using a visual culture and multimodal theoretical framework. Both within-case analysis (Merriam, 1998) and comparative analysis (Merriam, 1998) were completed. Following this, inferences and meaning constructions (Merriam, 1998) were undertaken based on themes arising (Miles and Huberman, 1994) between teachers and schools based on educators' lived experiences, teaching approaches, and learning through a comparison of educators' personal perspectives.

The two high schools: the formal learning environments

Both secondary schools studied are situated within a Canadian prairie city with a population of close to 700,000 people. The city has a vibrant film arts community featuring numerous film/video organizations at the local and provincial level. Professional filmmakers, directors, and actors from this city have become recognized at the international level and major films have been produced within the city such as *Capote* in 2005.

DOI: 10.1057/9781137475176.0008

The schools chosen for the research (Orangeville Collegiate Institute and Applewood Alternative High School) are very different educational institutions and were selected not only for their outstanding video/film programs but also because they are so unalike.

Orangeville Collegiate Institute is a mid-sized school, built in 1974, located in a middle class, economically privileged suburban district with approximately 70 teachers who teach in either the French (grades 9–12) or English (grades 10–12) programs. The school also offers a specialized *Advanced Placement* (AP) *Program* for those youths who are highly motivated academically. I focused on the English Program, as this is where the film/video program is situated. Students attending Orangeville have an equal ratio of males to females for a total of 960 students from numerous ethnic backgrounds.

Similar to Orangeville, Applewood Alternative has the same student gender balance and a film program, which begins in grade 10 and extends to grade 12. Concerning their differences, however, Applewood, founded in 1969, is approximately one-fifth the size of Orangeville, with only 11 teachers and a student population of 250, mostly comprised of an Aboriginal, at-risk population. Furthermore, Applewood is located in an inner city, and economically challenged community, and is solely an English School (grades 9–12) with no French Immersion or *AP Program.*

The mandates of both schools also vary. Orangeville is a comprehensive academic school with a humanistic, philosophical approach. Its primary focus is on academics and the development of student self-respect, dignity, confidence, social conscientiousness, duty, and the nurturing of critical thinking and decision-making skills. Although the administrators at Applewood also claim their mandate to be academic, in comparison to Orangeville's, it is clearly not. In reality, the mandate and primary focus of Applewood is to keep students in the program and have them graduate with a diploma and enter the workforce as active, contributing citizens.

Students and their parents choose Orangeville because of its superb sports and film/video programs and its high academic standing. Upon graduation, most students proceed to higher education. Contrasting to this, many students choose Applewood because they wanted to avoid what they had experienced in their former high school experience including ethnic exclusion, isolation, falling behind in learning, and bullying. Additionally, Applewood students contend with troubling issues at home or personal issues like drug use. Applewood teachers

DOI: 10.1057/9781137475176.0008

are trained to address their students' needs. Mr. Smith, the new media teacher at Applewood, affectionately calls his students, "*survivors*." Teachers at Applewood strive to provide individualized programming, address gaps in youths' learning, create a nurturing environment, and construct a personalized atmosphere for their students in order to motivate them, connect them to, and keep them in school.

The school program and curricula: Orangeville Collegiate Institute

At Orangeville Collegiate Institute there are two teachers in the new media program. One is trained in Visual Arts Education (Mr. Jamie Foster), and the other in Science/Geography (Mr. Sam Christo). Mr. Christo also has a background working in the film industry. The film program is specialized and has a focus on art: the technical aspects serving the artistic vision. The two teachers cover film theory/criticism, film/video production, film history, and film aesthetics, which aligns with discipline-based art education (DBAE)[4] situated in visual arts education (Bates, 2000). Mr. Foster designed the program and wrote curricula in line with provincial curricula mandates, and in doing so, utilized his visual arts background with a DBAE focus to form a strong foundation.

Prior to working at Orangeville, Mr. Foster started exemplary film programs at two other schools. Indeed, he won the coveted *Prime Minister's Award for Teaching Excellence* in Canada in 2001. When the principal of one of his former schools moved to Orangeville Collegiate, he quickly coerced Mr. Foster to begin the film/video program there in 2005. Working alone for the first two years, Mr. Foster then recruited Sam Christo, a former educational assistant in his previous school, to work as a certified teacher forming a close-knit team with him at Orangeville. Together they developed a notable program based on lecture, discussion, as well as group and independent work held both in and outside the classroom walls.

As part of new media program, Mr. Foster developed an additional focus on teaching animation and film special effects. Students are taught to use equipment ranging from the rudimentary to high-end including the expensive *Red* camera used in Hollywood that the Head of the Department strategically bought.[5] The program is designed to cultivate youths' technical and media literacy as well as their production and artistic skills. Student evaluation is undertaken by each of the two teachers using

DOI: 10.1057/9781137475176.0008

such traditional formats as rubrics, marking schemes, and tests. In creating the film/video program, Mr. Foster conceived of two streams both of which are student driven: one as *Filmmaking*; the other as *Independent Film*. For both streams, Mr. Foster developed and wrote his own extensive curricula and books for each grade level which came under the auspices of "specialized programming" at his school board level. The software students work on include iPhoto, iMovie, iStopmotion, Final Cut Pro, Photoshop, iDVD, Motion, Adobe After Effects, and GarageBand.

For the first stream on *Filmmaking*, Mr. Foster created three courses, one each for grades 10, 11, and 12. "*Filmmaking 1: Digital Filmmaking*," the grade 10 course, has a focus on the study, production, and the theory of advertisements, silent, action, and documentary films. "*Filmmaking 11: Animation*," the grade 11 course, has as its focus the production and theory of traditional, stop motion, and matte animations, as well as moving imagery using Flash software, and Rotoscoping. "*Filmmaking 111*," the grade 12 course, is centered on the production, appreciation, and theory of film and videomaking through examination of famous Hollywood films such as *Citizen Kane*, short, narrative, and experimental films with a particular focus on such theoretical areas as analysis of film mythology, story structure, dialogue, shot types, transitions, scriptwriting, and plot breakdowns (Figure 4.1). The courses are interrelated, each building

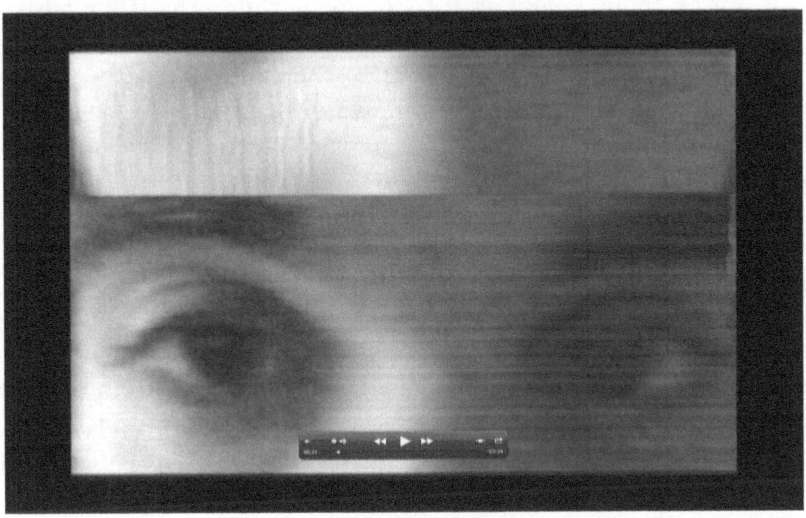

FIGURE 4.1 *Work by high school student from Orangeville Collegiate,* "Face"
Source: Video still: produced in the *Filmmaking 111* class.

DOI: 10.1057/9781137475176.0008

from the skills, concepts, and production techniques of the one before it. Mr. Foster employs educational scaffolding methods that work well within this programming structure. Moreover, he teaches skills required to prepare students to create a large film production: this directly relates to the "*Independent Film Program*" [IFP] stream. Without refined knowledge of, for example, animation titles and credits, feature length films would not look as sophisticated. This second stream prepares students to make top-quality feature films.

Feature length filmmaking production is the sole focus of the second stream called the IFP. Found in the curriculum booklet which students study, Mr. Foster (2011) writes,

> During the IFP course you will participate in advanced group based filmmaking experiences. It is our goal that you experience as much as possible the act of shooting a major film. By the end of the course you should have a greater appreciation for the work that goes into a successful narrative film. (Mr. Foster, personal communication, October 10, 2011)

Running a film, Mr. Foster explains, is really not about film but about integration and planning, and more planning. It is about developing student's organizational skills. The positive aspects of video study, he reflects, are that all students can participate, from the intellectual teenager who writes the scripts, to the artistic youth who is the DOP [Director of Photography], to the kinesthetic child, who is the busboy or works with lights. One 60-minute and over film is produced per year—an ambitious venture for any high school film program. Typically in most film programs, short video/films are preferred as the longer ones are harder to produce due to the time, money, and the massive coordination of roles.

As in the filmmaking stream, the IFP stream also involves a well-planned grades 10, 11, and 12 course. But, unlike the other stream, these courses in community film allow students from all grade levels to work together in an inter-age community. Additionally, a student in grade 10 can also take this course in grades 11 and 12, thus building her/his knowledge and skills and, significantly, often acting as a mentor to younger students as they graduate to the higher grades. Regularly, students who take the other, more individualized stream, also take this community stream, and are thereby immersed in filmmaking. For the IFP stream, the sole focus is a feature length film production. To this end, students

DOI: 10.1057/9781137475176.0008

work with their teachers on writing and developing a script which is then taken into film production and finally postproduction. Film shooting occurs in and outside the schools in a variety of locations sometimes hundreds of miles away from the school site and at all times of the day, night, and on weekends. Because of this, a flexible schedule is supported by school administration for both students and teachers involved in the film program.

For the IFP stream, students are divided into three groups for the entire year. Unlike traditional classes, the groups are not segregated by grade but by skill level. The first group is the *Technical Crew* comprised of youths trained for handling cameras, sound, lighting, editing, and other diverse film equipment. Students also learn about aesthetics and how it relates to technology. The second group is comprised of the *Crew Members* involved with such aspects as location scouting, crew call planning, acquiring permits, preparing food, budget, props, and makeup. This group facilitates the smooth creation of the film. The third group is the *Production Crew:* directors, writers, and actors who provide the theatrical component of any film venture. Three grade 12 students take the lead positions as directors of each of the three crews which work as a tightly knit community; often without the work of just one member, the production could not proceed. Such teamwork develops student responsibility and a type of learning interrelationship that has teenagers dependent on one another, which serves to develop interdependency and high intrapersonal engagement. As a former Squadron Commander in the Canadian army, Mr. Foster sees similarities in working on a film and working in the army and has drawn from his army experiences to shape his teaching. Mr. Foster provides an example:

> The army is just sort of like *juggling.* At first you're juggling your own personal skills, whether it's your rifle skills, your own personal hygiene, how to dig a trench, and stuff like that. Then you get into a leadership position and you're juggling all your own personal skills, but then you're managing three or four people...and then you're given a platoon of thirty people. I was only a Squadron Commander for two to three years. I was trained as a Captain for years...but all that training when you're in tank platoon you have upwards of two hundred and fifty infantry and carriers behind all of your tank platoon. You have T-33s [an American jet trainer aircraft) and F18s [a twin-engine supersonic combat jet] in the air and you're the Combat Team Commander and everybody is going off at your word. The

DOI: 10.1057/9781137475176.0008

> biggest thing you see is you've got all of these vehicles moving forward and if somebody takes a right turn, left turn, and moves and you're in the forest, you're backing up and moving all of those vehicles around it literally. It can take an hour and a half if you make one wrong turn and so what you start to sense is you get the sense of this momentum and how to communicate to a mass audience clearly enough and how to stop things from going off the rails fast enough that you can pull them back. It's the small details that screw you up through, whatever weird situation [you're in]... In the film world it prepares you for that kind of thinking where you're just constantly on top of things asking questions. (Mr. Foster, personal communication, October 3, 2011)

Mr. Foster elucidates further, offering another example of the way in which his army experiences have affected his teaching:

> The other big thing that we talked about was *liaison*... You're doing your planning of how this is going to come out. So for example, before if you're doing a night patrol, you've got your platoon dug in and you're night patrol usually leaves. Whenever a night patrol leaves everybody is in the trenches except for the people sleeping and then you exit. You go do your night patrol and then you come back at a predetermined time and everybody occupies the trenches who is awake because somebody's going to be following you back. That's the likely chance you're going to get into a firefight. Well weird things happen. Before you leave on a patrol you've got to do a test fire. Well if anybody hears gunfire then you do a "stand to" and everybody who is asleep wakes up and goes to the trenches... So what was happening is you know people don't liaise? They come to the platoon, they're in a rush, test fire weapons, everybody locks and loads, bang bang, "stand to," and everybody yells "stand to" in the trenches. Because nobody told them that there was going to be a test fire, all the people get up and they're only having two hours of sleep... That liaison gives you the situation where it's going off the rails. If I did this as a crisis, I need to tell this commander or this person that this is going to happen ahead of time or there's going to be a clash of people. Anyway those are the kinds of situations that really "prep" you... [In film production] you've got to communicate all the way down to the person who is managing the lights and setting the parking on the parking meters. You know, you've got to be making sure you've got tech crew parking or stuff like that... (Mr. Foster, personal communication, October 3, 2011)

From pre- to postproduction, many professionals from the film community are sought out to teach and train students at Orangeville.

DOI: 10.1057/9781137475176.0008

Teenagers are taken out of school to be instructed in the community and guest speakers are brought into the class. Professional equipment is rented for students' use. Mr. Foster is a successful grant writer and to date has raised approximately $130,000 for his program. He also brings in money through ticket sales to his regular school film festival screenings in which student works are shown to the entire school and school community. Moreover, student works are entered into local, provincial, national, and international film/video competitions, an exciting venture as students realize that a vast viewing audience will be seeing their new media productions (Figure 4.2).

The teachers of Orangeville's film/video program use social media to drive student motivation. Most finished student works are posted to the school's website and to YouTube, one of which received close to three million "hits" by July 2014, causing the young filmmaker to become a local media celebrity, interviewed by numerous local and national media in radio, television, and the news (Figures 4.3 and 4.4). A few students from Orangeville Collegiate actually do go on to pursue film within the industry, but it is noted that Mr. Foster does not actively promote this career choice. For Orangeville Collegiate students, careers in areas like

FIGURE 4.2 *Work by high school student from Orangeville Collegiate,* "Room"
Source: Video still: video exhibited at an international exhibition in Tallinn, Estonia (2011).

DOI: 10.1057/9781137475176.0008

FIGURE 4.3 *High school student from Orangeville Collegiate,* "Drums in the Snow"
Source: Video still from the YouTube video.

FIGURE 4.4 *High School student from Orangeville Collegiate,* "Lookout"
Source: Video still.

medicine, law, and engineering are promoted. However, overall, what makes the program at Orangeville Collegiate strong is that it is well developed and has an emphasis on training students in artistic theory and creative expression.

The school program and curricula: Applewood Alternative High School

Two people are involved in the video/film program at Applewood Alternative High School: one, Jasper Smith, the Head of the Department, began it in the early 1990s with an arts background in Drama Education; the other, Donald Dubiel, an educational assistant, focuses on enabling the technology to run smoothly.[6] Mr. Smith is a former professional actor[7] whereas Mr. Dubiel has a background in photography. Together they bring their experiences, knowledge, and skills to the classroom. Like Mr. Foster who brought in a close associate to establish an effective two-person team in the video/film program at Orangeville Collegiate, Mr. Smith, who had worked effectively with Mr. Dubiel in previous school film endeavors, brought him over to work at Applewood in 2003. Despite Mr. Dubiel's position as educational assistant, he positions himself in the role of the teacher and students respect and listen to him carefully. Splitting the duties, Mr. Dubiel works the technological parts of the program while Mr. Smith handles the artistic and educational part. With an avid interest in film and video, Mr. Dubiel trains students in digital media and assists them when faced with technical difficulties and challenges. Mr. Smith writes curricula, makes certain it meets the provincial curricula guidelines, and imbues the program with the artistic Drama, Film, and English Language Arts components. He also is responsible for the teaching.

To launch the new media program at Applewood, Mr. Smith sought professional advice from the provincial Film Training Organization. Additionally, he obtained a grant from Industry Canada to transform a classroom into a film studio. Unlike Orangeville Collegiate, at Applewood Alternative, the program focus is on new media production with a special concentration on hands-on learning using individualized instruction to suit each student's needs with considerable one-on-one learning. Often, though, group work occurs, especially during the production phase of filming. Students progress at their own rate through course materials and the class is mainly informal, wherein students work independently or within groups. When needed, Mr. Smith will give mini lessons to those students who need to learn the material. Oftentimes the classroom will be empty with students out working on a "shoot."

Building students' production, technical, and artistic skills are key for Applewood's program, and students are in control of their work from

DOI: 10.1057/9781137475176.0008

preproduction to postproduction. Developing these students' skills is focal to both programs, but unlike in Orangeville, at Applewood Alternative the theoretical, critical, and historical aspects of filmmaking are not the emphasis. Again, contrasting to Orangeville, which has teacher-driven evaluation, at Applewood it is negotiated between the teacher and the students through dialogue and is formed on an individual basis for each project undertaken. However, both schools have a student-driven focus. Likewise, the expectation that all students post their completed new media works to the school's website and on social media such as Facebook is common to both schools. At Applewood it is actually written in the curricula that the active presence of student artworks through the school website is a key expectation and this very act of Internet communications is embedded within the marking scheme. Like Mr. Foster's students, Applewood students learn how to work effectively with film, video, animation, and current software.

Applewood's new media program is comprised of three film/video courses written by Mr. Smith called "V*ideo Production*" for grades 10–12. However, unlike at Orangeville Collegiate, at Applewood there is only one stream. Mr. Smith devised this stream to be a combination of both Orangeville Collegiate streams. At the grade 10 level, the curriculum is comparable to Orangeville's *filmmaking* stream but at grades 11 and 12 level the curriculum is modified depending on what is planned by Mr. Smith to be either a class film project or independent work: this is similar to Orangeville's "*IFP*" or *Filmmaking* stream.

Comparable to Orangeville Collegiate, Applewood has evident scaffolding built into the curricula by Mr. Smith beginning at the grade 10 level. However, the curricula are notably less structured in grades 11 and 12. During grade 10, students learn about concept development, visual language, and technical skills. Youths begin the course by creating a picture story from still images.[8] Once they have mastered this first step, they proceed to create a 2- to 3-minute video in any genre, then explore mood or subject in another short video, and proceed to create a simple scene with a 2-person dialogue. Following this they produce a 2- to 3-minute documentary and then a short video exploring community concerns. As a result of these exercises, learners explore narrative and nonnarrative structures, how to convey meaning through both auditory sounds and visual images, and handle a variety of genres while learning to use video software and hardware. Specifically, students design new media projects using a range of media from video to animation to mixed digital media

DOI: 10.1057/9781137475176.0008

(Figures 4.5 and 4.6). Teenagers finish the course with a final 5-minute open-ended independent video production in any genre or style, and in narrative or nonnarrative productions. As discussed, grades 11 and 12 are far less structured and far more flexible and open-ended. At these grades, if a large project is set up by the teachers, grade 11 students can work for

FIGURE 4.5 *High School student from Orangeville Collegiate,* "Gates"
Source: Video still.

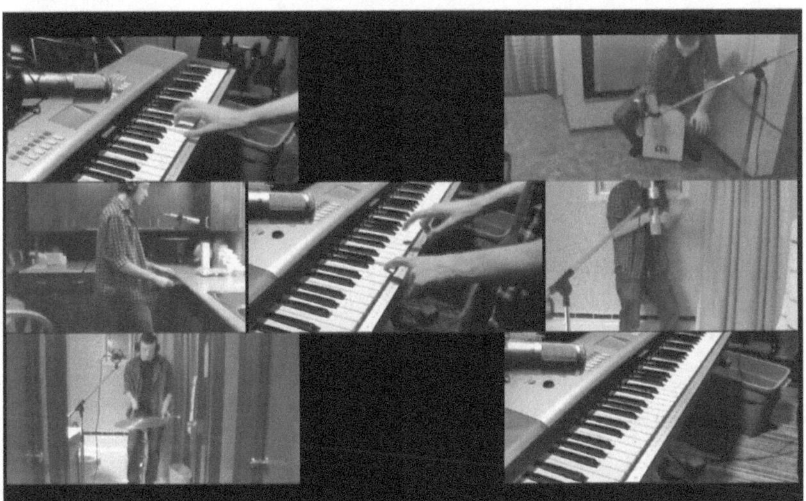

FIGURE 4.6 *High school student from Orangeville Collegiate,* "Music"
Source: Video still from the YouTube video.

DOI: 10.1057/9781137475176.0008

the entire year with grade 12 students, and so inter-age classes are established. Also, at this level, youths are expected to incorporate advanced digital techniques including blue screen and GarageBand, creating their own sound track for audio production. Moreover, at this level students assume responsibility for all aspects of their new media works, from being in charge of locations and equipment, to forging community partnerships with people and companies within the film industry, to taking control of casting and directing. In short, they oversee all aspects from preproduction to postproduction. At the higher level, the courses can be similar to Orangeville Collegiate's *Filmmaking* stream if students work on individualized and personal new media endeavors. Or the courses can be similar to Orangeville's *IFP*[9] if the project is one in which all the students are involved. Mr. Smith deliberately keeps the courses flexible at these higher grade levels to enable students to become involved with special projects occurring in new media from year to year. Projects vary from ones about provincial *Cancer Care* to ones about Aboriginal issues. For the latter, Mr. Smith sought the rights from the Steinbeck Foundation—a difficult feat in itself as the foundation does not offer these rights easily—to produce a movie based on the novel, *Of Mice and Men.* Applewood students adapted the book to the screen by writing their own film script. Drawing upon the First Nation's community, they recruited six professional Aboriginal filmmakers to help them. Students participated by adapting the novel to their own situation, delving into the First Nations' point of view through the scriptwriting process (Figures 4.7 and 4.8). There were three months of filming alone and the entire process extended over years from its initial stages to completion as a grades 11 and 12 combined classroom community venture with international screening in major film festivals. Mr. Smith explains that,

> When things are really cooking and you're on set and you're out on location and there's the whole thing going on, it's pretty exciting, but the logistics of it can be a bit of a nightmare. It's a big train that just keeps moving. If it stops then you're in trouble so it just has to keep moving otherwise you're wasting gigantic amounts of money. (Personal communication, January 3, 2011)

Mr. Smith actively plans for feature length, large-scale works, which he calls *authentic* experiences as he feels they are similar to ones in the film industry. Mr. Dubiel claimed to overhear film industry professionals\ working with students on an Applewood production say it was more like a professional film than a high school production. The Applewood filmmaking experience not only conjures up a real filmmaking situation, but

DOI: 10.1057/9781137475176.0008

FIGURE 4.7 *High school student from Applewood Alternative School,* Video DVD Cover, of Mice and Men
Source: Video still.

FIGURE 4.8 *High school student from Applewood Alternative School,* George from of Mice and Men
Source: Video still.

DOI: 10.1057/9781137475176.0008

it creates real life pressure for students as well. Mr. Smith explains that "People have to perform and people have to be there, and if they are not there you know the shit hits the fan, and yes it can be very volatile even at a professional level" (Personal communication, January 3, 2011). In Mr. Smith's class, students working on a large-scale new media venture will work together in a tight-knit group. They are interdependent on one another, which is similar to the Orangeville approach. According to Mr. Smith, this is the most significant area of focus in film: the social aspect and the building of team skills. Student engagement is high, as is their responsibilities toward this project. He says:

> Students realize filming is bigger than themselves but at the same time they're part of a team and they have to be there because they're part of the crew and we're the professionals showing them you're the boom operator and you're the sound engineer so together you guys have got to get the sound. You still have to give the kids a lot of encouragement and you have to talk to them about that responsibility because they will still go out that night if their friends call. So wake up calls are needed. But you know when you think of it, even professionally, there's a lot of transportation involved.... Okay the actor is staying at this hotel and the director is here. You pick them up at quarter to. You think, "Do they need a wake up call?" So you have to logistically bring people together. We did that and you get a routine: go and wake up the director and have a coffee for him and the kid comes stumbling out and off you go to the location. Students say about the filmmaking experience that, "I learnt what team work is and learning how to work with people and about responsibility."... A lot of those kids were really committed to that project, *Of Mice and Men* and they were as focused as they've probably ever been in anything they had done... So that's really what they're learning more than anything else. I mean yes there are the skills that they're picking up which are certainly important but it's the personal skills, the team skills that are bigger somehow. Cause those you know you can apply all the time... (Mr. Smith, personal communication, January 3, 2011)

Mr. Smith and Mr. Dubiel work with at-risk students who often have trouble staying in school so it is not uncommon for them to hunt down their students at youth's homes to remind them of their obligations toward the project. However, most often the students are motivated, take responsibility for the project, and meet the challenge as evidenced by the success of the department's multitude of video/film prizes which celebrate student films that win international, national, and local awards. Entering their work in competitions, Mr. Smith observes, drives the students (Figure 4.9).

DOI: 10.1057/9781137475176.0008

FIGURE 4.9 *High school student from Applewood Alternative School,* Train
Source: Video still.

As in Orangeville Collegiate, Mr. Smith reaches out to the community in significant ways, getting professionals in the field of new media to give speeches within the schools, training students, and having students visit these professionals within the community. Directors, actors, and sound engineers often volunteer their time to act as mentors, establishing one-on-one relationships with Applewood students.

Additionally, youths learn about animation and video using software similar to those discussed at Orangeville. Equipments used are standard video cameras, iPads, and sound mics used in many video programs across North America; however, Mr. Smith does not buy such high-end cameras as the *Red* camera purchased by Mr. Foster. Like him, though, Mr. Smith will seek out sophisticated equipment from film companies on a borrow/rent basis. Two professional film/video organizations within walking distance of Applewood are regularly used. Mr. Smith accesses grant money from Industry Canada and the Network of Schools; he also writes independent grants for the purchase of equipment and software, and provides honorarium for guest speakers.

Mr. Smith and Mr. Dubois have focused on having the film/video program work seamlessly in order to integrate it with other school programs. Teachers in other subject areas often ask the film students to create a new media work for class credit, which Mr. Smith and Mr. Dubiel

DOI: 10.1057/9781137475176.0008

help facilitate, such as scriptwriting for an English credit or making a documentary on the planet earth for a science credit. Educators work together with students to make this cross-curricular partnership easy, and it is evident that students are highly motivated to communicate their learning through moving imagery rather than through more traditional communication vehicles such as essays and reports. Overall, at-risk learners at Applewood Alternative are highly motivated by new media production with its emphasis on artistic production and have made successful careers within the film and new media industry.

In particular, Orangeville and Applewood curricula differ in their emphasis on aesthetics, production, technology, criticism, history, and theory. In the case of Orangeville, teachers placed an emphasis on all of the above, whereas the emphasis at Applewood is on aesthetics, production, and technology. Therefore, the curricula in Orangeville tend to be more academic whereas at Applewood it is shaped by the needs of at-risk students and the schools' mandate to integrate subject matter. Despite this, they share numerous similarities in the new media curricula. For instance, both Mr. Smith and Mr. Foster outreach to the community to enrich their teaching content; both place an emphasis on art as the foundation of their program; both write and develop their varied program to meet the needs of teachers, students, parents, and administration. In particular, both curricula enable independent and community new media production at each school.

Teachers and their pedagogical approaches: a comparison of Applewood and Orangeville

Similarities

Further on the topic of similarities, it is also found that educators at both schools are ready and willing to tackle emerging new art domains and multimodal learning. Mr. Foster and Mr. Smith began working with analogue technologies in the 1990s and they have adapted to the developments in digital technologies that occurred within the last 20 years. They developed the educational, artistic, and technical sides of new media. In the case of Mr. Smith, who preferred to develop artistic and educational aspects, he sought an expert within the field to handle the ever-changing digital technologies within his classroom. Both models are successful.

DOI: 10.1057/9781137475176.0008

At Applewood and Orangeville, the teachers' roles are flexible and diverse. Mr. Smith and Mr. Foster act as guide, lecturer, and director at various times within the same class. In their classes, formal lecture structure, group learning, and individualized learning occur depending on the subject matter. Pedagogical approaches are flexible, ranging from student to teacher-centered. This corroborates with the findings of Gray and Macgregor (1987, 1990) who, in their studies of high school Canadian art teachers, found that their roles within a class could range from "engineers, executives, directors or consultant" (1987, p. 29) depending on what role they needed to assume at the time. This is also similar to the educational technology researcher, Cuban (2001), who in his study of American technology classrooms found that teachers using technology also took on various other roles as required. In all these cases, collaboration is evident: teachers teach students and students teach students in informal group learning environments. In addition, in other research studies of other schools pertaining to the use of digital technologies in other classrooms (Black, 2002, 2009a, 2009b) it was found that students often teach their teachers about new media. However, I rarely encountered a student teaching his/her teacher at either Orangeville or Applewood, owing to Mr. Foster's and Dubiel's high degree of self-taught technological knowledge.

Differences

Pedagogical approaches differ between the Applewood and Orangeville programs; Mr. Foster and Mr. Christo at Orangeville rely on a step-by-step teaching approach, using a planned pedagogical process. They use booklets Mr. Foster wrote for each grade and program and proceed through these with flexible guidelines. Often they lecture to students and have classroom discussions, as well as have students work in groups and independently. The approach at Applewood is different. Youths will learn software and hardware as needed: for example, if students envision a special animation effect or the layering of multiple images which they want to incorporate into their work, they first have to learn it (Figure 4.10). Rather than moving from chapter to chapter in a production book on videography or being taught step-by-step techniques of filmmaking by a teacher, Applewood students learn technology on a needs basis through the act of artistic envisioning and creation. Both teaching processes work well and are effective within their respective programs.

DOI: 10.1057/9781137475176.0008

FIGURE 4.10 *High school student from Applewood Alternative School,* Street Scene
Source: Video still.

Relationships

At the two schools student/teacher relationships are emphasized. Mr. Foster is looked upon by his students as a hardworking, dedicated, extremely knowledgeable educator. Indeed others have described him as charismatic. At Applewood, Mr. Smith also nurtures student/teacher relationships. Students look upon him as a caring, flexible, kind teacher who has expertise within the field of education and within drama, drawing upon his experience as a professional actor and integrating his expertise into the film classroom. Mr. Smith explains:

> Whenever I'm working with a student or a group of students and it involves character, I bring some of that knowledge into the picture whether it's the students writing dialogue, we'll talk about what dialogue is, and if it's verbose and artificial, we'll talk about subtext—talk about what characters don't say... If we're on set and people are acting we'll talk about realistic acting versus caricatures, so I'll get into character, acting with them, when we'll discuss a scene and talk about how an actor can approach a part in terms of its arc. So, the whole range of what it is behind the character [namely] motivation, intention and all those kinds of things will come into the picture. (Mr. Smith, personal communication, October 3, 2011)

DOI: 10.1057/9781137475176.0008

Mr. Smith is well liked by his students and creates a warm, nurturing, easygoing classroom environment.

Negotiations with school administrators

Teachers in both formal learning environments have attained flexibility within the school. Mr. Foster successfully negotiated with his school administration for students to be able to take time off regular scheduled classes provided they work extra hours on course content—this is highly unusual within a formal school setting. He demands that both he and his students work weekends and school nights to make a film successful. Mr. Foster expects students to tackle difficult work with dedication and motivates them to meet his expectations. In one instance, when I was expecting to observe his class, I found the classroom empty because the students had worked throughout the weekend and consequently, in light of this, Mr. Foster had negotiated with his administrators to cancel regular classes. Likewise, Applewood's students are involved in film shoots during nights and weekends. As long as Mr. Smith engages at-risk students within the film program, the administration is supportive. In this way, both Mr. Smith and Mr. Foster have managed to break down traditional learning environment structures.

Conclusions: learning from effective practices

Differences are evident between Orangeville Collegiate Institute and Applewood Alternative High School: namely, the curricula and some aspects of their pedagogical approaches. These differences support the view that there is no *right* way to teach new media; in fact, successful media programs do not have to duplicate each other; it is the richness and complexity inherent in these programs that make them unique. Still, the programs also have marked similarities that aid in developing effective and successful practices, as noted and discussed, which can assist in the development and strengthening of any new media program. **Firstly**, *practical approaches* are utilized at both schools, ranging from pedagogical approaches, teacher roles, to curricula structures. At both Orangeville Collegiate and Applewood Alternative Schools, teachers have established the program so that knowledge and skills are scaffolded. It also shows that

DOI: 10.1057/9781137475176.0008

teamwork is beneficial in new media programs, as both Mr. Foster and Mr. Smith quickly sought out others to support their visions and programs. Furthermore, these teachers also write their curricula to meet the needs of their students, administrators, and school communities. In addition, Mr. Smith and Mr. Foster engage in diverse teaching approaches, readily changing their roles for the task at hand. Similar to Gray and Macgregor (1987, 1990) who concluded in their research that teachers perform multiple roles in art education, it was also found in this research regarding the teaching of new media that educators act as facilitator, instructor, project director, grant writer, artist, and negotiator. Furthermore, both recreate actual professional film production, which requires dedication and hard work, in school hours and beyond. However, doing so requires plenty of money. In fact, money is key and acquiring fiscal support to strengthen the new media programs at both Orangeville and Applewood is of utmost importance. Mr. Smith and Mr. Foster accept the fact that part of their job is to write grants, win awards, and sell tickets for school film screenings, and do so consistently from year to year.

Secondly, breaking boundaries of *formal school structures* is successfully undertaken and achieved at both schools. Mr. Smith and Mr. Foster have worked toward flexibility in terms of (a) curricula structure and pedagogical approaches; (b) breaking down grades to merge students together in different age groups and class levels; (c) giving credit in other disciplines for work undertaken in the new media program; and (d) working within and outside of school hours. This, of course, means that both other teachers and school administration have to be supportive of the new media programs for the flexibility to work.

Thirdly, students of Orangeville and Applewood alike not only learn about new media but also about *developing life skills*. This is particularly apparent in the group filmmaking focus at both schools wherein students work in large groups, much like in a film company production. For the making of feature films, youths rely on each other in a very complex, interdependent manner, promoting student responsibility, interpersonal relationships, and an extremely strong level of "focus" required for the project to be successful. At both schools these requirements promote a high level of student engagement in all aspects of the program, from the digital and social to the creative dimensions. Teachers likewise work toward developing student trust and respect of others within their classrooms and the relationship is reciprocal between students, teachers, and their community. As a result, the following life skills are nurtured

DOI: 10.1057/9781137475176.0008

in both new media programs: (1) taking responsibility toward others; (2) engaging in, focusing on, and developing extreme concentration in their new media work at all stages of development; (3) taking ownership of what they produce and feeling pride in excellence; (4) developing interpersonal and intrapersonal skills including juggling duties and responsibilities; and (5) learning how to collaborate and liaison with others. Both Mr. Smith and Mr. Foster believe that these qualities are the real outcome of what is being taught and are invaluable to students in all their endeavors and subject areas—in effect, personal and social skills that will help them throughout their lives.

Fourthly, *art drives both programs*. Both Mr. Smith and Mr. Foster attempt to develop divergent thinking, creative learning pedagogy, and creative art production through their curricula and teachings (Figure 4.11). Mr. Foster and Mr. Smith are both trained in the arts, and make art the foundation of their new media. Although technical aspects are important in their programs, technology actually plays a decidedly secondary role. For Mr. Smith and Mr. Foster, the goal is to nurture creativity and personal expression through students' study of new media. Emphasis is placed on artistic theory, aesthetics, and open-ended curricula frameworks to foster students' imaginations through various

FIGURE 4.11 *High School student from Applewood Alternative School*, "I Went to War 2"

Source: Video still.

DOI: 10.1057/9781137475176.0008

means such as showing professional artistic works as exemplars, asking students pertinent artistic questions, and holding to the expectation that no two video works be the same, but will in fact be student driven, self-expressive, and thus unique. Although different approaches and curricula are set at each school, learning at both schools is established so that students are taught aesthetics and artistic practices that enable them to use technology to make their work personally meaningful. Thus, learners develop rough artistic ideas that they work through to fruition in their final artworks. Mr. Smith explains this, stating that, "The focus has been about working on projects for the students. It's not about the technology you know: the technology is a means to an end. It's about projects. I know other schools you're learning a skill... whereas the point [at our school] is to create something" (personal communication, January 3, 2011). As Gouzouasis (2006) points out, technology must be informed by the arts—that the arts communicate and make technology meaningful. We see the arts infusing the digital medium with artistic expression in significant ways. The analogy is given that without the arts, new media works are lifeless and mechanistic, similar to prefabricated houses; with an arts-focused curricula, new media production becomes uniquely designed architectural structures—the latter being far superior.

My perspective corroborates with Buckingham (2007) who notes a gap or "digital divide" between student technology usage in and outside of formal learning environments. He advises educators using digital technologies in all disciplines to be cognizant of the ways in which youths are using technology outside of school, and advises teachers to develop student digital knowledge and usage within their own classrooms to improve technology access and "allow more opportunities for open-ended, creative uses of media" (p. 98).

Fifthly, creativity[10] is evident in Orangeville's and Applewood's new media programs, meaning specifically to nurture students' curiosity, resourcefulness, willingness to experiment, and problem-solving skills, and to develop their originality. The ability for students to attempt artwork that is new, to take risks, to fail and fail again until the work meets their vision or successfully converts into another, and to transform the known to the unknown is highly significant. Essentially, a way to nurture creativity is through allowance of student play, and both Mr. Smith and Foster actively promote this in their classes. In concurrence, Rogers writes that creativity,

DOI: 10.1057/9781137475176.0008

> Is the ability to play spontaneously with ideas, colours, shapes, relationships—to juggle elements into impossible juxtapositions, to shape wild hypotheses, to make the given problematic, to express the ridiculous, to translate from one form to another, to transform into improbable equivalents. (Rogers, 1962, p. 68)

Out of this play ensues inventiveness as well as tolerance for ambiguity.

Sixthly, at both schools the *teachers engage their community* so that students are often working in professional organizations and with professionals in the new media industry: conversely, these experts are often found speaking at, guest teaching in, and working within both Applewood Alternative and Orangeville Collegiate schools. Both Mr. Smith and Mr. Foster engage a network of organizations and professionals within the new media field. Having experts teach both informs the students and teachers and enables both Mr. Foster and Mr. Smith to strengthen their curricula with new, strong, valuable content. Moreover, both teachers agree that having experts teach engages and motivates youths.

Both Mr. Smith and Mr. Foster make certain to outreach to communities from the international to the local level. The process of achieving this is embedded in their programs: teachers submit final new media student works to new media communities and students post their works on the school website and on YouTube and Facebook, thus promoting digital practices so that teenagers' voices contributing their own digital narratives will be heard within an international community. The result of these actions is that students learn not only from their teachers but also from their peers, and from professionals within the industry. These relationships also enable student recognition for their outstanding works on a level not possible even 25 years ago.

Seventhly, it is noted that Mr. Foster and Smith *construct very careful, well-planned curricula that are scaffolded to build students' skills and knowledge*. These are not programs in which teachers merely hand a camera to students and tell them to make a video or new media project: in neither program is the so-called simplistic *point and shoot* approach[11] to teaching video taught. To this end, youths at both schools work within the expectations of the program and curricula set. Within this formalized structure they discover personal determination in choosing content, in working with the technology, and in creating their new media works. As Leonardo da Vinci observes, "Art lives from constraints and dies from freedom" (The Painter's Keys, 2014).

DOI: 10.1057/9781137475176.0008

Responding to da Vinci's truism, Mr. Smith and Mr. Foster establish parameters within the new media project, stipulating the time required for completion, the genre, and other specifics, as do educators in traditional art classrooms. Latitude is given to the students to write or cowrite scripts along with their teachers, create props, act, film, and edit. Within set boundaries there is a great deal of student autonomy to explore, to choose, to play, and to create. Teenagers work within a project-driven, student-centered, project-based learning environment in which assignments are nonprescriptive and open-ended.[12] Mr. Foster and Mr. Smith both require students to problem solve: learners must decide what their new media assignment will be and how they must go about achieving their vision.

Lastly, *students are given the freedom to formulate and communicate their artistic ideas* in all aspects of new media production: personal vision is indeed nurtured. Youths are given free reign (provided the material is not racist, sexist, or offensive) to be creative. Both Mr. Smith and Mr. Foster have structured their film programs so that the students experience filmmaking derived from their own personal experiences, thoughts, and creative ideas and are able to share these within an international community (Figure 4.12).

FIGURE 4.12 *High School student from Applewood Alternative School,* "I Went to War 3"

Source: Video still.

DOI: 10.1057/9781137475176.0008

Final thoughts and recommendations

Overall, Mr. Foster and Mr. Smith are educators who are self-sufficient, independent, and willing to learn and adapt multimodal learning in our ever-changing digital world. Moreover, they write effective, art-based curricula, placing art as a foundation in new media curricula which specifically targets their particular, unique educational situations. It is noteworthy that the one key, overriding vision both teachers share is not only to teach new media but, most importantly, to develop their students' life skills: in both their programs, technology plays a definitively subsidiary role. In their teaching Mr. Smith and Mr. Foster seek autonomy as teachers, engage their community, employ differing flexible teaching styles, and place great value upon their relationships with students to nurture youths' creativity and self-expression. Significantly, both are willing to reject models and rules that do not work for them while continuing to innovate and formulate new working models that significantly strengthen their programs within their formal learning environments.

It is recommended that school administrations at the board and school levels become knowledgeable about the needs of educators and their new media programs. By revealing the complexity of teacher practice through these two case studies, it is hoped that school administrators are willing to ensure their support and provide infrastructure in order to create quality new media programs in public schools. Pedagogical approaches and teaching methods differ between Applewood and Orangeville: however, in both schools it is found that teachers require flexibility and financial and institutional support. One of the reasons the programs at both schools flourish is because the administration and other teachers are flexible and supportive; this is crucial in order to allow new media programs to thrive.

It is also recommended that educators be given more autonomy and regarded as producers and managers of change in our digital world. Through the thick description of this research, it is hoped that teachers and educators can envision how teaching with digital technologies can be realized and how obstacles can be resolved in their own unique contexts. In the case of Mr. Smith and Mr. Foster, they are keen, skilled, and dedicated teachers who are allowed to develop effective curricula drawn from their own and their staff's varied interests, skills, knowledge, and expertise. Because of this, the curricula are effective. Furthermore, they design a curriculum to meet the needs of their students, their

DOI: 10.1057/9781137475176.0008

community, the parents, and their particular school. Due to this, course content is strongly supported by all involved. The pedagogical approach breaks away from those of more traditional school systems. I agree with Gray and MacGregor's conclusions (1987, 1990, 1991) that teachers' personal qualities are key to student success and as such, educators should be regarded as *critical transformative agents* (1987). These authors strongly state that to "hire a teacher is to hire a curriculum" (1987, p. 133). My findings corroborate these findings: specifically that well-developed programs, customized curricula, and engaging pedagogy are derived from dedicated teachers and their teaching and this should be embraced rather than stifled in formal learning environments. Buckingham (2007) corroborates with this stance: in addressing higher education he writes, "...like the university it should be staffed by professionals, who have the power to make their own decisions about how the business of education should be carried out.... [This is a stance clearly positioned against the] government view of teaching as a matter of 'delivering' an externally defined curriculum" (p. 183). Rather than have a "top-down" curricula imposed upon educators from governments at the federal or local levels, it is strongly advised that new media education become flexible, develop and support individual teachers, and nurture their programs within our formal learning environments.

Furthermore, in agreement with Buckingham (2007), it is recommended that the arts model be embraced by educators working with new media in other subject areas such as English, sciences, media, and history. The conditions necessary for quality teaching and learning in new media are those of skilled art educators who work with new media as an art form. Strong, creative educational digital practices are developed by teachers who foster students' self-expression, youths' unique voices, creative visions, through film production, and, ultimately, through a thorough and sophisticated knowledge of new media as an art form.

Applewood Alternative High School and Orangeville Collegiate Institute offer two different models that have evident similarities. Both these new media programs are strong, are recognized, and work. What is found is that youth engagement within both film programs is impressively high. Both school models offer insight into curricula development and pedagogy, the importance of fiscal and artistic concerns, flexible programming by the administration, and the significance of nurturing

DOI: 10.1057/9781137475176.0008

teacher/student autonomy. It is hoped that the ideas discussed can affect the decisions of educators and educational administrators in regard to the fostering of new media practice within and beyond the arts at the secondary school level in our public schools.

Notes

1 At the middle school level the teachers worked within common generalist programs as is typical in North American public schools. Hence digital studies at this level were not as fully developed as those at the secondary level. This is the reason the focus is on high schools in this chapter.

2 Originally four schools (two middle and two secondary schools) and eight educators were involved with this study; however, due to limiting the focus of this paper on high schools, two schools and four educators are discussed. For a discussion of the creative use of digital technologies at both the high and middle school levels refer to Black's article (2014).

3 To showcase the effective practice of art teacher educators, the criteria for this choice were based on the following: (1) recognition of the schools by professionals in the field of education (specifically educators and administrators at the university level and within provincial professional new media and art education organizations); (2) media coverage of students' and teachers' successes; and (3) students of the program being recognized and receiving awards for their art projects on an international, national, and local basis.

4 Discipline-based art education (DBAE) is a movement emerging from the United States in the early 1960s and it was financed primarily by the Getty Institute. Adherents of DBAE incorporate the teaching of art production, history, criticism, and aesthetics within the K-12 curriculum.

5 Mr. Foster has online discussions with famous film directors, one of which was about whether the *Red* should be used in high school film education classes. He advocates for its use stating youths need to be trained on superb equipment; the directors, however, state that kids need to use more rudimentary equipment in training.

6 The traditional role of an *educational assistant* within Applewood's school board is that of assisting educators with special needs' students. However, Donald Dubiel has been able to position himself to meet the needs of the film program at Applewood.

7 Mr. Smith has worked with such notable actors as the internationally renowned actor, Christopher Plummer who starred in such films as *The Sound of Music*.

DOI: 10.1057/9781137475176.0008

8 This technique of teaching in which students are asked to move from working with the still image to the moving image is a part of old European film schools' curricula as described by the director Roman Polanski in his biography (Polanski, 1984). Mr. Smith is well aware of Mr. Foster's program and vice versa. I observe that there has been much healthy competition between the two educators. They are cognizant of what each other has undertaken, implemented, and achieved.

9 For a further discussion of creativity refer to Black and Browning's article (2011).

10 A point and shoot approach is one in which the teacher merely asks students to film. The teachers do not, therefore, teach film grammar, theory, history of film, aesthetics, nor the working out of stages from preproduction to postproduction.

11 This approach as described above is common in visual arts classrooms (Bates, 2000).

References

Bates, J. K. (2000). *Becoming an Art Teacher*. Belmont, CA: Wadsworth.

Black, J. (2002). *Topsy-Turvy Teacher-Student Relationships: An Examination of Digital Multimedia Teaching and Learning* (Doctoral dissertation, University of Toronto, 2002). *Dissertation Abstracts International, 63*, 6.

Black, J. (2009a). Case study research: three model visual arts new media programs in Canadian secondary schools. *Journal on Education, Informatics and Cybernetics, 1*(3), 1–6.

Black, J. (2009b). Necessity is the mother of invention: changing power dynamics between teachers and students in wired art classrooms. *Canadian Review of Art Education, 36*, 99–117.

Black, J. (2014). Model new media/video programs in arts education: case study research. *The International Journal of Education and the Arts, 15*(6), 1–26.

Black, J. & Browning, K. (2011). Creativity in digital art education teaching practices. *Art Education, 64*(5), 19–24 and 33–34.

Buckingham, D. (2007). *Beyond Technology: Children's Learning in the Age of Digital Culture*. Cambridge, England: Polity Press.

Cuban, L. (2001). *Oversold & Underused: Computers in the Classroom*. Cambridge, MA: Harvard University Press.

DOI: 10.1057/9781137475176.0008

Denzin, L. & Lincoln, Y. (2000). *Handbook of Qualitative Research*. Thousand Oaks, CA: Sage Publications Inc.

Gouzouasis, P. (2006). Technology as arts-based education: does the desktop reflect the arts? *Arts Education Policy Review, 107*(5), 3–9.

Gray, J. & MacGregor, R. (1987). PROACTA: personally relevant observations about art concepts and teaching activities. *Canadian Review of Art Education, 14*, 23–33.

Gray, J. & MacGregor, R. (1990). PROACTA 11: personally relevant observations about art concepts and teaching activities (Eastern Canada). *Canadian Review of Art Education, 17*(2), 130–135.

Gray, J. & MacGregor, R. (1991). A cross-Canada study of high school art teachers. *Canadian Journal of Education, 16*(1), 47–57.

Jenkins, H. (2009). *Confronting the Challenges of Participatory Culture: Media Education for the 21st century*. Cambridge, MA: MIT Press.

Manitoba Education. (2014). Grade 9 to 12 Visual Arts: Manitoba curriculum framework of outcomes—Draft. Manitoba: Manitoba Education.

Manitoba Education and Training. (1988). *Art 100, 200, 300*. Manitoba: Manitoba Ministry of Education.

Manitoba Education and Training. (1990). *Curriculum Support Series: Art Evaluation Guidelines k-12* (ISBN 0-7711-0941-5). Manitoba: Manitoba Ministry of Education.

Manitoba Education and Training. (1993). *Senior 1 Art: Interim Guide* (ISBN 0-7711-1162-2). Manitoba: Manitoba Ministry of Education.

Merriam, S. B. (1998). *Case Study Research in Education: A Qualitative Approach*. San Francisco, CA: Jossey-Bass Inc.

Miles, B. & Huberman, A. (1994). *Qualitative Data Analysis*. Thousand Island, CA: Sage Publications Ltd.

Morin, F. (2010). *A Study of Arts Education in Manitoba Schools* [Monograph, vol. 3]. Manitoba: Manitoba Education Research Network (MERN).

Polanski, R. (1984). *Roman by Polanski*. New York, NY: Ballantine Books.

Rogers, C. (1962). Toward a theory of creativity. In J. S. Parnes & H. F. Harding (Eds), *A Sourcebook for Creative Thinking* (pp. 63–73). New York, NY: Charles Scribner's Sons.

Shulman, L. S. (2007). Practical wisdom in the service of professional practice. *Educational Researcher, 36*(9), 560–563.

DOI: 10.1057/9781137475176.0008

Stake, R. (1994). Case studies. In N. Denzin & Y. Lincoln (Eds), *Handbook of Qualitative Research* (pp. 236–247). Thousand Oaks, CA: Sage Publications Inc.

Stake, R. (1995). *The Art of Case Study Research*. San Francisco, CA: Sage Publications Inc.

The Painter's Keys. (2014, July 29). Leonardo da Vinci quotes [Web log post]. Retrieved from http://www.art-quotes.com/auth_search.php?name=Leonardo+da+Vinci.

Weisshaar, L. (2012). The peaceful village: a message from the executive director. *Report of the Manitoba School Improvement Program*. Retrieved from www:msip.

Yin, Robert. (2003). *Case Study Research: Design and Methods* (3rd edn.). Thousand Oaks, CA: Sage Publications.

DOI: 10.1057/9781137475176.0008

5

Learning in Place: Profiles of Youth Media Arts Practices in an Informal Learning Setting

Ching-Chiu Lin and Kit Grauer

Abstract: *This chapter presents practical understandings of how media arts education programs in an informal learning setting offer an alternative pedagogical space to engage youth through creative media production opportunities. By sharing our research findings from the fieldwork drawn from the Gulf Islands Film and Television School (GIFTS) on Galiano Island in British Columbia, Canada, we identify the qualities and characteristics of media arts practice in the context of informal learning spaces that help foster a relational understanding of youth creative endeavors and digital participation. Rather than examining the specific competencies that participants have achieved at GIFTS' youth media programs, we highlight the pedagogical moments that have taken place throughout the process of learning and its contexts.*

Keywords: art education; arts learning; community-based art education; informal learning; place; video production; youth

Black, Joanna, Juan Carlos Castro, and Ching-Chiu Lin. *Youth Practices in Digital Arts and New Media: Learning in Formal and Informal Settings.* New York: Palgrave Macmillan, 2015. DOI: 10.1057/9781137475176.0009.

As young people's lives are increasingly mediated by digital technologies, media arts—such as documentary and other technologically supported art forms—help young people develop an understanding of the world and how they fit into it. This chapter presents practical understandings of how media arts education programs in an informal learning environment offer an alternative pedagogical space to engage youth through creative media production opportunities. In particular, we offer findings from a multiyear research project on community-based media arts education initiatives, presenting the fieldwork drawn from one of our research sites, the Gulf Islands Film and Television School (GIFTS) on Galiano Island in British Columbia, Canada.[1] By sharing our research findings, we aim to identify the qualities and characteristics of media arts practice in the context of informal learning spaces that help encourage young people's creative endeavors and digital participation.

The place of GIFTS

Founded by documentary and commercial filmmakers on the site of a former remote logging camp, GIFTS is a community-based media arts educational center on the island of Galiano in British Columbia, Canada. Isolated by geography, Galiano Island is situated across the Georgia Straight from the Mainland. It is one of a series of small islands that are strung across the American/Canadian border in the Salish Sea and make up the San Juan Islands to the south and the Gulf Islands in Canada. The island itself is about 26 kilometers long with a population of less than 1000 permanent residents.

Providing in-residence programming, GIFTS offers courses ranging from youth media workshops to adult and teacher professional development courses that are structured around conceptualizing, collaborating on, and producing films in the span of one to two weeks. Participants are invited to work in small teams with professional filmmakers, addressed as mentors, to produce short films featuring such genres as drama, documentary, and animation. They are immersed in an environment of cooperative, collaborative, and creative practice, mirroring experiences of the professional film industry. The basic filmmaking equipment and editing programs are

DOI: 10.1057/9781137475176.0009

seen as professional tools and treated with respect; participants are treated as filmmakers and taught to use professional language, tools, and techniques.

For a typical one-week media program, participants arrive on Sunday evening on the last ferry of the weekend from Vancouver. It is a 40-minute ferry ride across the Strait of Georgia, a picturesque landscape of mountains, ocean, and the Southern Gulf Islands in the distance. Picked up by a rickety school van at the ferry terminal, students are taken through the rainforest into the middle of nowhere where they experience darkness and silence in a closed space with other uncertain participants. Leaving the comfort of their familiar lives, clutching their pillows, clothes, and possessions, participants have described the Sunday ferry and bus rides like a Harry Potter trip to Hogwarts as they journey into the unknown.

Awaking in an unfamiliar dorm bed next to newly met roommates, on Monday the students finally are able to see where they are located. Surrounded by an extensive and lush second growth rainforest, GIFTS' campus features a large courtyard surrounded by student dorm rooms, a kitchen, and several classrooms made out of shipping containers. Usually George, the founder of GIFTS, meets the students at the common courtyard area; he orients the group and introduces the mentors while trying to make students more at ease in this new place. George explains that for the remainder of the week, students will work with mentors with various expertise—acting, directing, documentary, drama, and animation—to create a short film or animation in groups that is then shown to family and friends through a film screening event. In other words, the curricular premise of GIFTS is to produce a short film in a week. There is no fixed block scheduling at GIFTS except the mealtimes, yet the compressed timeline creates a sense of urgency as the participants' films will be screened publicly at the end of each program. Commenting on this model, George said, "Creating an environment that is goal-oriented also means there's a real responsibility that each person has to make it work. We can't delay the public screening" (George, personal communication, August 2009).

George's orientation usually does not make students feel better. In fact, the pressure of working with strangers on a tight production deadline creates an odd and silent moment for the start as students have expressed mixed feelings about such requirements. When time becomes the constraint, the collaborative process of working together in groups challenges students' familiar learning patterns: block schedules, individual

DOI: 10.1057/9781137475176.0009

assignments, deadlines, and rubrics. They are asked to communicate with others, to work through arguments and conflicts, and to have each other's voice heard respectfully.

George then directs the entire group to the large wooden clock with the timeline of the GIFTS curriculum painted on its face outside the main classroom (Figure 4.1). The clock is an obvious reminder of the constraint of time, as well as the accountability and responsibility assumed by the fluidity of the curriculum structure. Knowing students' discomfort, George would point to the clock saying, "It's the deadline you need to work against, not each other." During our observations on mentors' interaction with students, time was always referred to as a reason to work through problems, tensions, and even fatigue, as Peter, a mentor, observed,

> Those kids live it and they're here 24-7. So it's that concentrated energy and the time for critical and creative expansion. You can quickly cut to the chase and facilitate magic that does, in fact, happen here. But I really think it's that intensity of making a film in a week. My favorite is the visual reminder: the clock. (Peter, personal communication, August 2009)

The setting of GIFTS dislodges a participant from a familiar context, such as home or school, bringing into relief an individual's existing way of knowing in relation to a multitude of other ways of knowing. Questioning "the stability of the *what* dimension of knowledge," Thomas and Brown (2011) observed, "Reframing knowledge as a *where* question underscores the increasing importance of context" (p. 93). Having a place that resets habituated interaction and social structures around a shared interest enables participants to, in a sense, reinvent themselves in relation to each other as filmmakers. Such an experience highlights the fact that participants learn meaning constriction through the *where* dimension rather than simply through the *what* dimension of making films in isolation. George also reflected on the significance of the place of GIFTS,

> It's just a configuration of many things that have come together. The whole experience starts with the ferry, then getting picked up at the ferry with some rattly old vehicle, and then coming to an old logging camp where kids can't go off. It's very levelling, so that no matter where you've come from in your life, we are all humbled here. There's no pretension. It creates the environment that is out of ordinary, so that allows people to reinvent themselves. [Students] don't know anybody, they don't have any peer groups, so they can be anyone they want to be. (George, personal communication, August 2009)

DOI: 10.1057/9781137475176.0009

The experience of GIFTS

Participants at GIFTS

GIFTS draws youth learners aged 12–20 from urban areas across the Pacific Northwest and remote communities in Northwest Territories. Learners participate either because of their own interest in digital media or on adult recommendations from acting agencies, parents, teachers, or First Nations Bands.[2] Some are recommended by their schoolteachers due to the lack of media programs in public schools, whereas some First Nation communities fund their young people with a return mission of piloting digital learning networks. There are also participants from different socioeconomic and cultural backgrounds whose communities have made program attendance possible through self-nomination for scholarships. There are fees for those who can afford to pay, and many intern possibilities and funding opportunities from special interest groups and agencies are available for youth with an interest but no other means of support.

We have observed that GIFTS' programs tend to attract young people who are falling out of the education mainstream, and some of them have returned at least twice. For example, Alex, an aboriginal young man, returned three times to the Aboriginal youth media program specifically because he felt he achieved more through GIFTS' programs; he said,

> At GIFTS, they teach you everything that you need to know right away. I wouldn't want to stay in college for years. Here, I learned immediately what it takes to actually make a movie and how to work the camera right away, how to direct your actors, how you learn the editing process right away as opposed to years of training in college. (Alex, personal communication, October 2011)

Ben, a homeschooled young man who also had been to GIFTS three times, commented on his GIFTS experience, "I just do things at my own pace...I like our mentors would just leave us alone with the camera" (Ben, personal communication, October 2011). Danielle, an Aboriginal high school dropout, described why he returned, "I really enjoy the freedom of letting me do what I want...It wasn't the product of what [mentors] told us to do. It was the product of what we want to come up with" (Danielle, personal communication, August 2009). Unlike other first-time participants experiencing the unfamiliarity, these young men returned to GIFTS knowing that the program structure complemented their learning style and comfort level. As Ellsworth

DOI: 10.1057/9781137475176.0009

(2005) observed, "By cultivating acknowledgements and awarenesses of experiences of our learning selves, we might become capable of relating to certainty not as its own guarantee but as an emergent quality of movement/sensation" (p. 161). This type of learner at GIFTS strives to negotiate differences where points of connection emerge from their sense of certainty, stemming from increased learning comfort with the surrounding. Alex commented on why he came back for another intake,

> I was really interested in the Aboriginal program because I thought [at GIFTS], I'd have a better chance to write my own scripts about certain issues affecting Aboriginal people. I think I'd have a lot more in common with people in this program...I definitely feel like I related more to the people here last time and that definitely helped me in the process of making the movie. (Alex, personal communication, October 2011)

Liam, a senior mentor commented on this return phenomenon:

> The reason why these kids come back is because they have a good time here...there are no grades at GIFTS; nothing is mandatory here. Some kids care about the product, but some are more interested in socializing and that experience itself. I think it's the fun and enjoyment that keep them coming back and make them remember it. (Liam, personal communication, August 2009)

Mentors at GIFTS

Mentors at GIFTS are professional filmmakers, college students, or professionals working in the film industry. Staying away from titles such as teacher, instructor, or trainer that may indicate power and authority in a learning context, a mentor's role at GIFTS is much closer to that of facilitator or mediator. As Thomas and Brown (2011) observed, "Mentors provide a sense of structure to guide learning, which they may do by listening empathically and by reinforcing intrinsic motivation to help the student discover a voice, a calling, or a passion" (p. 51). Mentors at GIFTS draw from their professional experience to ask technical questions, to describe the conditions students are working under, and to point out the possibilities and challenges of how students might bring their ideas to the screen. They value their relationships with students from a perspective of recognizing each individual's strength through collective endeavors. At the same time, they strike a delicate balance between making sure ideas are

DOI: 10.1057/9781137475176.0009

heard while ensuring there is movement toward the group's production goals. We have seen the role of mentor as managing producer in the film and television industry, one who resourcefully oversees the execution of production.

GIFTS' mentors usually did not have much to say about either their teaching philosophies or pedagogical approaches, since such terms might sound like jargon to them. In interviews with mentors, they described not coming into workshops with their own predetermined agenda. Instead they focused not on what they could do to prepare for specific concepts or themes, but on how they could respond to the ideas initiated and developed through dialogue with students. Warren, a veteran mentor, claimed, "My job is to help students work together to commit to their own ideas in a collective" (Warren, personal communication, October 2010). Another mentor Allison remarked,

> I try to get my hands off, and just let students take the reins and take control of their production. I just need to be there to sort of facilitate so that students know what's possible and what's available for them, to their advantage of making their films. (Allison, personal communication, October 2010)

In particular, many mentors working at GIFTS are alumni who took a course at GIFTS as preteens or teens and returned as interns and mentors while studying in colleges or working in the film industry. Over time, they have established an interest-driven network in which they share common experiences and give back to GIFTS as a collective. Allison, a mentor who had not been a student at GIFTS, observed this return phenomenon,

> I'm one of the few exceptional mentors who did not have any connections with GIFTS. There's a lot of mentors and interns who have been students of GIFTS, and there's a sort of progression of coming here as a student and becoming an intern and then eventually mentoring and that sort of evolution. (Allison, personal communication, October 2010)

Nick and Derek, both former GIFTS students and now mentors, feel it is hard to describe why they returned. Nick, a freelance animator introduced to the world of animation at GIFTS when he was 16, said, "I just keep coming back every year. I can't explain it" (Nick, personal communication, October 2010). Derek, a college student majoring in Film Studies, remarked, "I really enjoy the simple, solitary learning experience [at GIFTS]" (Derek, personal communication, October

DOI: 10.1057/9781137475176.0009

2010). Jeremy, currently an intern and former participant who wants to become a mentor, described his reason for returning to GIFTS:

> Why people keep coming back is because you come here for one week and time just goes out the window. For example, I already feel like I've been here a week, but I've been here just two days. Time is... Time is longer. I feel like I'm getting more stuff done here. (Jeremy, personal communication, August 2009)

Relational encounters with GIFTS

Media arts education programs outside of school contexts offer arenas of learning for young people to respond to the challenges of interpreting, understanding, and participating in the world of constant change. Educators have suggested that such learning experiences provide an effective mechanism for young people to build individual skill sets, promote community engagement, and offer broader social benefits (Halverson, 2010; Peppler, 2013). Scholarly evidence shows that youth engagement in the process and production of digital media opens avenues to discuss issues such as empowerment, voice, activism, and literacy proficiency (Buckingham, 2011; Poyntz, 2009). While recognizing the significance of such issues in young people's digital-mediated learning experience, views of youth creative practices have been marked by an increasing turn to contextual and intersubjective understandings of digital participation and meaning construction (Thomas & Britton, 2012; Underwood, Parker, & Stone, 2013). Although prescriptive accounts of goal-driven focus on developing youth competence are convenient for framing outcomes up to a point, they risk becoming formulaic and may fall short of individuals' learning potential. This concern demands that we understand the complexity of young people's relationships with creative media production as engagements of serial encounters that "open up the possibility of new ways of thinking about who we are in relation to others and in relation to place" (Davies, 2009, p. 5). As learning is imbued with social relations, GIFTS' focus on creative media production allows young people to foster artistic, interpersonal, and responsive encounters with media products they produced, with others and with the environment. Rather than externally prescribed, a relational understanding of such actions permits us to capture pedagogical moments that enable a continuous process of unexpectedness that provokes new possibilities.

DOI: 10.1057/9781137475176.0009

Next, we turn to the perspective of relationships to discuss further the learning experiences at GIFTS.

Encounters with others

As digital media are an increasingly inescapable fact of life for many young people, their engagement in media production and consumption can be understood as *participatory cultures*, which media scholar Henry Jenkins and his colleagues defined as "a culture with relatively low barriers to artistic expression and civic engagement, strong support for creating and sharing one's creations, and some type of informal mentorship whereby what is known by the most experienced is passed along to novices" (Jenkins et al., 2006, p. 3). In keeping with Jenkins, we have observed that, as participants of participatory cultures, GIFTS learners' learning and sharing around digital media move beyond merely peer assistance to form peer-to-peer mentoring relationships. As Ellsworth (2005) observed, "media...have the potential to deliver open-ended and indeterminate sensations, movements, affects, thoughts, action, and interactions in and across societies with pedagogical consequence" (p. 126). Young people's creative media practices—through sound, graphics, movements, and multimodal combinations—provide opportunities for conversation with their peers and enable new ways of representing voice, knowledge, and experiences of individuals. Since GIFTS' program structure sets the tone through teamwork and cooperation, the interplay between the collective nature of participation and the social nature of media production shapes the nonhierarchical relationships among students, interns, and mentors that result from interest-driven learning. The "some type of informal mentorship" in Jenkins' term, is fluid, evolving, and unstructured at GIFTS; it helps to keep up the momentum of projects and to drive individual's commitment to a group effort. Participants at GIFTS expressed positive comments on mentors' open-mindedness to their ideas and working styles, as well as the realization that the constraints of time and space allow them to follow their passion through peer interaction and self-directed learning.

For example, a team of three teens made a documentary on the topic of online gaming from one of the youth media programs. Anna was an Advanced Placement student heading to a university for film studies; Blake, a self-taught musician; and Danielle, an Aboriginal high school dropout. They were a cast of unlikely partners but grew to understand

DOI: 10.1057/9781137475176.0009

the strengths that each other brought to the film. Reflecting on his experience, Danielle commented,

> The mentors gave us some directions or techniques and then they would leave us alone. Our mentor, he sort of flipped to work for us, not for us to work from him. At school, we were working to the teachers' standards and their expectations and ideas. When I am here, really the mentors are there to help us get our vision out. (Danielle, personal communication, August 2009)

While asked to summarize her experience for friends, Anna described,

> It's really cool to see how you can bend facts to your views, how we come up on film as a team, and a finished project of your idea and your vision. [This experience of making a documentary] makes me realize that your idea is not just your imagination, but your actual thoughts and beliefs can come up on film, and it's just an amazing sight to see. (Anna, personal communication, August 2009)

Commenting on how their team worked to complete their film, Blake said,

> We were encouraged to try out different things, so we all had a little bit of a shot with editing, directing, or shooting. But as it turned out, we all experimented in that and we all went back to what we were interested in, in the first place. (Blake, personal communication, August 2009)

When asked to elaborate his role in the making of this documentary, Blake explained with his teammates' strengths in mind, "I enjoy doing sound mixing and Photoshop stuff, but I learned from Danielle a lot about filming angles and from Anna, she taught me how to get organized." Anna also reflected on her working experience with the two,

> I think we had a really good group. The film is really about three parts: the shots you get, how to clip it together and the music that's put in. Danielle, holy crap, some the camera shots he got were amazing. And Blake's music was original...he meshed the music with the visual effects seamlessly and everything was working out just the way we wanted it to...We managed to pull it all together by having just the three of us. (Anna, personal communication, August 2009)

The intensity and forthright insight that Anna brought to explaining the collaboration between the three, especially her support of Danielle and Blake, speak volumes about the need to have diverse groups of students work together to discover their own talents as well as appreciate the uniqueness of others. When learners take on an active role in learning

DOI: 10.1057/9781137475176.0009

from and with their peers, a sense of collectiveness emerges. "Collectives are not solely defined by shared intention, action, or purpose... Rather, they are defined by an active engagement with the process of learning" (Thomas & Brown, 2011, p. 52). In the case of GIFTS, the collective takes shape through multilayers of participation in media production, social relations, identity construction, and friendship formation. Reflecting on his experience at GIFTS, Tom, a grade 11 student, said, "The whole experience was a lot better than just the end movie" (Tom, personal communication, October 2010). It suggests an alternative form of pedagogy that shifts away from seeing interest-driven youth media work as detached entities to underline "a move towards recognizing the continuous becoming" (Massey, 2005, p. 21) in which the learning relationship is foregrounded.

At the same time, while GIFTS derives its energy and strength from relational encounters with others, the collective is not limited to an engagement around youth interests in digital media. Rather, its affective, empathic, and reciprocal relations play a critical role in forging the collective at GIFTS. Reflecting on the assets of GIFTS, George said,

> One of the things I love is the camaraderie and the acceptance of the people, especially in the youth programs, the acceptance of the weirdoes. The weirdoes here are cool. People in the nerd hole are cool; cool is redefined at GIFTS. It's not your normal cool. It's not the kids with the most gadgets or the best clothes. It's cool because of their personality, interesting ideas, or the ability to pull the team together... they learn to accept and respect each other. (George, personal communication, August 2009)

Encounters with the environment

Considering young people's complex relationship with media, media education is undergoing a shift from analyzing media text to engaging in media production for meaning construction and social action (Goldfarb, 2002; Poyntz & Hoechsmann, 2011). This shift calls attention to close connections between youth media production and remix culture in reflecting a contemporary condition that young people's relationships with media manipulation are factors by which messages are carried.[3] It indicates that meaning, constructed through means of digital media, "arises not from interpretation... but from contextualization" (Thomas & Brown, 2011, p. 95). This is because young people learn key concepts like audience, representation, and narrative along with techniques and

DOI: 10.1057/9781137475176.0009

ideas for crafting context, such as remixing, appropriation, and adaptation in media education. Through processes of making media content and restructuring context, young people learn through the act of play, a form of learning that involves engagement in imagination, experimentation, unexpectedness, trial and error, and practice (Buckingham, 2009; Gee, 2010; Ito et al., 2008; Sefton-Green, 2011). Rather than seeing *play* as taking part in activities without seriousness, we agree with Thomas and Brown (2011) that "Play is the central tool for inverting the traditional hierarchy of learning and knowing" (p. 117). At GIFTS, play takes place through participants' relationships with the unique environment. That is, a merger between making and playing occurs when time and space are allowed for learners to mess around with equipment and tools, enabling them to nurture ongoing negotiation and communication throughout the production process, to resolve arguments and take feedback in a collaborative working atmosphere, and to hang out alone or with others on a daily basis in GIFTS' living-in media programs.

For the mentors, much of the teaching happens in the first few days in conversation with participants, which reinforces the notion that collaboration and communication are essential to conceptualizing, designing, and producing films. Mentors use the vocabulary and procedures found on professional film sets when communicating with participants and hold them accountable for the outcome. In interviews with GIFTS learners, many noted that being treated like professionals in the film industry enabled them to role-play a culture of filmmakers and to experiment autonomously and act on the responsibilities assigned to different roles. A sense of play forms slowly and grows subtly at GIFTS as learners engage not only in experimentation with techniques of film production but also in exploration of the social dynamics of their learning experience.

For example, in an Aboriginal youth media program, a group of teenage boys shot a ton of footage for their film and hung out in the woods for the most of daytime, burning the midnight oil to edit their film on the last two nights. A quiet young man from the Northwest Territories who regularly wore headphones and watched videos on YouTube at the kitchen corner turned out to have been working on remixing songs for a four-minute-long film. A grade 8 girl who signed up for the acting program hung out with every group and volunteered to be the actor if needed, and took a long walk to the beach everyday to practice alone. In one occasion, a group that needed to film a hillside chase scene asked other groups to help out. Dropping their tasks in hand, the entire intake of participants got on a crowded bus, eager to assist. Perhaps some just wanted to get away from the campus, whereas others were interested in playing roles on a film set. While filming, some were goofing around and joking with each other; others took their roles seriously setting up equipment or practicing lines. That afternoon, a group of youth who barely knew each other had developed as a collective through the involvement of an unfolding activity. They bonded through the moments of laughing, role-playing, hanging out, or shooting repeatedly.

Our field observation shows that the shape of learning at GIFTS is unstructured, evolving, and unpretentious, revealing "forms of experimentation and social exploration that are generally not characteristic of educational institutions" (Ito et al., 2008, p. 2). As GIFTS participants are held accountable to follow their interests and learning styles, such an experience allows learners the autonomy to foster and elicit a sense of ownership and control over their creative productions. Thus, this process of learning shifts from simply representing an experience to calling attention to forms of embodiment, seen as "a moving relation with forces, processes, and connections to others in ways that are unforeseen by consciousness and unconnected to identity" (Ellsworth, 2005, p. 121). As learners' embodiment is situated in specific arenas of learning, we may consider GIFTS a pedagogical space that is characterized by its "thrown togetherness" in which various factors are coming together to create a particular "here-and-now." As Massey (2005) argued,

> What is special about place is not some romance of a pre-given collective identity or of the eternity of the hills. Rather what is special about place is precisely that thrown togetherness, the unavoidable challenge of negotiating a here-and-now...and a negotiation which must take place within and between both human and nonhuman. (p. 140)

"Thrown togetherness," in a sense of GIFTS, means being treated like adults, as well as being forced into a situation where participants are expected to finish their films in a week for the public screening. While asked to describe his initial impression about GIFTS, Joel, a participant in the Aboriginal youth media program, put it, "Honestly I felt trapped. I can't go off anywhere or do something else. If I were in the city, I would be gone by now" (Joel, personal communication, October 2010). GIFTS participants are brought together to work through the challenges and tensions that the pressures of time and resources create in ways that simulate the realities of the film industry or any real-life scenario. Such

DOI: 10.1057/9781137475176.0009

constraints result in bringing creative tension, imagination, and uncertainty to the forefront throughout the whole process of learning, yet it also creates the conditions for taking risks to trust, communicate, and negotiate ideas of personal and collective significance. That is, recognizing the constraints as possibilities becomes a place of encounter where the interconnectedness of learning and body is evoked and marked "by its own indeterminacy and by its openness to an elsewhere and to an otherwise" (Ellsworth, 2005, p. 122).

Final remarks

Informal learning sites, such as community centers, libraries, or a place like GIFTS, offer a "third arena of learning," (Heath, 2001, p. 10), where learners seek opportunities to fulfill an interest-driven need that they often cannot achieve from home or school settings. In this chapter, we focus our discussion on the realm of out-of-school learning, and through our research, we describe how GIFTS offers an opportunity to better understand what pedagogical potential is enabled. Rather than examining the prescriptive principles or specific competencies that participants have achieved at GIFTS' youth media programs, we highlight the pedagogical moments taking place throughout the process of learning and its contexts. As artist Suzanne Lacy reminded us, human relationships are vital to young people's arts experience: "Youth development and education through art are essentially relational practices where we must assess the quality of these relationships in order to understand the effectiveness of the work" (2010, p. 230). Through the lens of GIFTS as an informal site of learning, we may see the importance of fostering a relational understanding of youth creative endeavors and digital participation that is unfolding, evolving, and emerging. That is, youth media production is not merely an end, but a means of social practice for cultivating relationships with the self, others, and the world, in which points of connection emerge through dialogue, collaboration, and interaction.

Notes

1 Over the past few years we have written on the various perspectives of this research: the conceptual basis of community-based media arts programs

DOI: 10.1057/9781137475176.0009

in reframing teaching and learning (Darts, Castro, Sinner, & Grauer, 2010); program implications for educational professionals in the public sector (Castro & Grauer, 2010; Lin, Castro, Sinner, & Grauer, 2011); case studies of how pregnant teens developed self-esteem and felt empowered through media arts learning experiences (Levy & Weber, 2011a, 2011b); digital storytelling as reflective art practice (Sinner, 2010); and pedagogical implications drawn from community-based sites of learning for art education (Grauer, Castro, & Lin, 2012; Lin, Grauer, & Castro, 2011).

2 In Canada, many First Nations Bands provide education funding to members of their communities. Both urban and rural Bands send participants to GIFTS in programs specific to their own interests (e.g., the Aboriginal Film Program) and/or to regular programs (e.g., the Summer Media Intensive Program).

3 Navas (2008) defined remix culture as "the global activity consisting of the creative and efficient exchange of information made possible by digital technologies that is supported by the practice of cut/copy and paste" (para. 5).

References

Buckingham, D. (2009). "Creative" visual methods in media research: possibilities, problems and proposals. *Media, Culture & Society, 31*(4), 633–652.

Buckingham, D. (2011). Youth media production in the digital age: some reflections—and a few provocations. In J. Fisherkeller (Ed.), *International Perspectives on Youth Media: Cultures of Production and Education* (pp. 375–379). New York, NY: Peter Lang Publishing.

Castro, J. & Grauer, K. (2010). Structuring democratic places of learning: The Gulf Island Film and Television School. *Art Education, 63*(5), 14–21.

Darts, D., Castro, J., Sinner, A., & Grauer, K. (2010). New media arts educations: how community-based programs can reshape teaching and learning in the age of Web 2.0. In R. Sweeny (Ed.), *Inter/Actions/ Inter/Sections: Art Education in a Digital Visual Culture* (pp. 80–89). Reston, VA: National Art Education Association.

Davies, B. (2009). Introduction. In B. Davies & S. Grannon (Eds), *Pedagogical Encounters* (pp. 1–16). New York, NY: Peter Lang Publishing.

Ellsworth, E. (2005). *Places of Learning: Media, Architecture, Pedagogy.* New York, NY: Routledge.

Gee, J. P. (2010). *New Digital Media and Learning as an Emerging Area and "Worked Examples" as One Way Forward.* Cambridge, MA: MIT Press.

DOI: 10.1057/9781137475176.0009

Goldfarb, B. (2002). *Visual Pedagogy: Media Cultures in and beyond the Classroom*. Durham, NC: Duke University Press.

Grauer, K., Castro, J., & Lin, C. (2012). Encounters with difference: community-based new media programs and practices. *Studies in Art Education, 52*(2), 139–152.

Halverson, E. R. (2010). Film as identity exploration: a multimodal analysis of youth-produced films. *Teachers College Record, 112*(9), 2352–2378.

Heath, S. (2001). Three's not a crowd: plans, roles, and focus. *Educational Researcher, 30*(7), 10–17.

Ito, M., Horst, H., Bittani, M., boyd, d., et al. (2008). *Living and learning with New Media: Summary of Findings from the Digital Youth Project*. Cambridge, MA: MIT Press.

Jenkins, H., Clinton, K., Purushotma, R., Robison, A., & Weigel, M. (2006). Confronting the challenges of participatory culture: media education for the 21st century. MacArthur Foundation. Retrieved from http://www.macfound.org/media/article_pdfs/JENKINS_WHITE_PAPER.PDF.

Lacy, S. (2010). *Leaving Art: Writings on Performance, Politics, and Publics, 1974–2007*. Durham, NC: Duke University Press.

Levy, L. & Weber, S. (2011a). "Yes, I am a mother and I am also a teenager": teen moms use digital photography to share their views. *Girlhood Studies: An Interdisciplinary Journal, 3*(2), 129–139.

Levy, L. & Weber, S. (2011b). Teenmom.ca, a community arts based new media empowerment project for teenage mothers. *Studies in Art Education, 52*(4), 292–309.

Lin, C., Castro, J., Sinner, A., & Grauer, K. (2011). Toward a dialogue between new media arts programs in and out of Schools. *Canadian Art Teachers, 9*(2), 24–37.

Lin, C., Grauer, K., & Castro, J. C. (2011). "There is nothing else to do but make films": urban youth participation at a film and television school. *International Journal of Education & the Arts, 12*(SI 1.8). Available at http://www.ijea.org/v12si1/.

Massey, D. (2005). *For Space*. London: Sage.

Navas, E. (2008). Remix: the bond of repetition and representation. Retrieved from http://remixtheory.net/?p=361.

Peppler, K. (2013). *New Opportunities for Interest-Driven Arts Learning in a Digital Age*. New York, NY: The Wallace Foundation. Retrieved from http://www.wallacefoundation.org/knowledge-center/arts-education/

DOI: 10.1057/9781137475176.0009

key-research/Documents/New-Opportunities-for-Interest-Driven-Arts-Learning-in-a-Digital-Age.pdf.

Poyntz, S. (2009). "On behalf of a shared world": Arendtian politics in a culture of youth media production. *Review of Education, Pedagogy and Cultural Studies, 31*(4), 365–386.

Poyntz, S. & Hoechsmann, M. (2011). Not just philosophizing: producing effective youth media and communication projects. In J. Fisherkeller (Ed.), *International Perspectives on Youth Media: Cultures of Production and Education* (pp. 301–316). New York, NY: Peter Lang Publishing.

Sefton-Green, J. (2011). Creative digital cultures: informal learning beyond the school. In J. Sefton-Green, P. Thomson, K. Jones, & L. Bresler (Eds), *The Routledge International Handbook of Creative Learning* (pp. 244–252). New York, NY: Routledge.

Sinner, A. (2010). Digital storytelling as art practice: a case of informal learning. *Arts and Learning Research Journal, 26*(10), 1–19.

Thomas, D. & Brown, J. S. (2011). *New Culture of Learning: Cultivating the Imagination for a World of Constant Change*. Lexington, KY: CreateSpace Independent Publishing.

Thomas, V. & Britton, K. (2012). The art of participatory video: relational aesthetics in artistic collaborations. In E. Milne, C. Mitchell, & N. De Lance (Eds), *Handbook of Participatory Video* (pp. 208–222). London, UK: AltaMira Press.

Underwood, C., Parker, L., & Stone, L. (2013). Getting it together: relational habitus in the emergence of digital literacies. *Learning, Media and Technology, 38*(4), 478–494.

DOI: 10.1057/9781137475176.0009

6
Conclusion

Juan Carlos Castro

Abstract: *In this chapter, the authors summarize the recurring themes from each chapter and propose considerations in regard to creating conditions for engaging digital media arts programs in and across informal and formal learning environments. The authors have found that effective new media pedagogy and curricula in both public schools and alternative settings share commonalities. These are: an offering of professional level skills, a supportive community of learners, an incorporation of youth's cultural practices, experienced teacher-professionals, and an emphasis on community engagement. The authors conclude this requires extraordinary leadership to support both students and teachers in these programs.*

Keywords: community; curriculum; leadership; new media programs; pedagogy; professionalism; youth cultural practices

Black, Joanna, Juan Carlos Castro, and Ching-Chiu Lin. *Youth Practices in Digital Arts and New Media: Learning in Formal and Informal Settings.* New York: Palgrave Macmillan, 2015. DOI: 10.1057/9781137475176.0010.

DOI: 10.1057/9781137475176.0010

It should be evident to the reader of this book that the characteristics of high-quality new media arts education in informal and formal settings look uncannily similar. As Sefton-Green (2014) has aptly described, the dichotomy between formal and informal educational settings is many times misleading. Instead, what is essentially a "political construct" (Sefton-Green, 2014, p. 187), is rather a differing set of social, cultural, and institutional practices. What is striking about each case of new media art curricula and pedagogy presented in the preceding chapters are the innovative strategies employed by educators that are contingent on a number of shared conditions and attitudes. By focusing on the shared characteristics that emerged in contexts ranging from at-risk youth community programs to film programs in affluent public schools, we argue that high-quality new media arts curricula and pedagogies can flourish in any institutional context with the appropriate conditions.

In this concluding chapter, we seek to outline, from our collective analysis, the following characteristics and the support necessary for each program's success. We set out to answer the question posed in Chapter 1: "Do these diverse educational experiences have pedagogical and curricula commonalities?" However, we are not interested in generating a list of best practices that when faithfully followed will result in pedagogical success. Instead, we acknowledge, on the one hand, the distinct populations, contexts, and challenges each case presents, and yet, on the other hand, we acknowledge that each case has shared characteristics that create the conditions for a high level of engagement for the learners participating in each program. Specifically, we are able to identify the following characteristics as shared between programs: (1) a commitment to teaching the professional craft of new media production; (2) the presence of a community of learners; (3) the incorporation of youth's cultural practices into creative practices; (4) the crucial pedagogical role of the teacher; and (5) a practice of connecting the curriculum to the community beyond the physical structure of the school or community center. While we are able to identify the above shared characteristics as essential features of each program's missions and practices, we also acknowledge that each new media arts program faces unique challenges.

The conditions necessary to foster meaningful engagement on the part of the student are as diverse as the individuals participating in these learning formal and informal environments. We are able to ascertain critical elements, from the above characteristics, as: leadership, from both educators and administrators, who are equipped to address the

DOI: 10.1057/9781137475176.0010

needs of their varied contexts combined with a commitment to adaptive innovative pedagogy and curriculum. The kinds of creative behaviors practiced by new media arts professionals require a commitment from both educators and administrators to create spaces that foster the characteristics identified.

Professional practice and identity

Students who study new media art can identify professional skills and equipment. Youth are savvy consumers of popular visual culture and are capable of recognizing when new media is crafted at a high level. Offering youth the means to craft works that resemble those made by professionals provides strong intrinsic motivation. In each case studied there are clear examples that point to youth describing how learning through professional processes and practices have empowered them by providing tools to articulate ideas in sophisticated ways. It is the act of adopting professional behaviors and seeing the outcomes of engaging in such behaviors that an individual's identity transforms. The process of transformation from consumer to producer is a powerful pedagogical event. In those instances of new media arts programs that serve marginalized youth, this act of identity building and transformation is an essential pathway for broader educational engagement across learning sectors.

Professional technical processes and equipment, however, alone are not enough. We observe across the cases studied that an essential feature of teaching professional-level new media arts production is teaching the process of production. Specifically, students are introduced to how professionals work together, communicate, plan, research, produce, reflect, and disseminate. At the Gulf Islands Film and Television School (GIFTS), presented in Chapter 5, students are taught to work together as a team, learning tools for collaboration and communication as used on professional film teams. In Chapter 4, students at both school-based film programs are given the duties of a filmmaking team and the responsibilities that come with each role. Students are expected to fulfill their duties as professionals, which means seeking the right to use copyrighted material, planning for shoots at all hours of the day, and meeting with local community members to orchestrate filming—these are just a few examples. And in Chapter 3, students have witnessed first-hand how their instructors, who themselves are practicing artists, use social media

DOI: 10.1057/9781137475176.0010

tools to disseminate their new media productions. Not only do they observe this activity, they are also encouraged to engage actively with disseminating their work.

In each of the cases presented in this book, there are no written curricula that outline how one should teach in a systematic manner. Instead, the curriculum is modeled on how new media arts production works in the professional fields of filmmaking, television, photography, and sound production. The teachers in each program draw from their professional experiences of new media arts production and construct their curricula. There is something to be said with providing a space for youth to take the responsibilities of a professional as they are held accountable to their learning. Accountability is not toward the teacher, but rather it is a responsibility toward their production team and the work itself. Students would often describe the feeling of responsibility to their peers as they work together toward a common goal such as the complete film, sound work, animation, video, exhibition, and submission to an international, national, and/or local film festival. As a result a culture of professionalism emerges.

Learning community(ies)

Identity development and performance of individuals have marked an impact on the learning of youth participating in the programs presented. Rather than the creative process being about individual expression and identity development through a visual media, the kind of identity formation reported in these studies is fundamentally shaped by the relationship linkages of the individual to the group identity. In other words, the kind of identity development undertaken as a result of participating in a professional new media arts production team initiates a strong sense of self that is connected to a lager scope of various forms of community. This is not to say that individuals lose themselves in the collective efforts of the group, but rather students are able to describe their unique contributions, while recognizing they have a synergistic effect on the outcomes of the group's productions. Students understand the distinction between their singular identity and their team's identity. Thus, the participating youth's ability to describe individual and collective contributions indicates the significance of peer-to-peer learning that occurred throughout the production process.

DOI: 10.1057/9781137475176.0010

In Chapter 2, Lin describes how the social nature of new media arts production contributes to the cultivation of learning communities that blur the boundary between students and instructors. Youth develop trust with each other as they coordinate action, communicate ideas, create interdependencies, and negotiate differences in intentions. As these kinds of relationships and knowledge production evolve, young people learn to work collectively through social action and creative endeavor. In both of the public school programs studied by Black in Chapter 4, youth grew interdependently through inter-age communities. For example, students in the 10th grade work with students in the 12th grade, setting up a form of mentorship and collective memory that transfers and evolves through successive academic years. At GIFTS, described in Chapter 5, a number of alumni of the program return after working in the professional field of filmmaking to teach future generations. Positive social relationships are so important to administrators and instructors at Maison Kekpart, as illustrated in Chapter 3, that it is an essential mission for school engagement and retention. The communities of learning fostered collectively are critical to keeping at-risk youth in school and youths engaged in learning and motivated throughout the formal and informal sites presented in this book.

Cultural and creative practices

As mentioned earlier, youth are particularly adept at consuming popular visual culture. They also have a desire to create works that have the look of professional production. Further, youth also seek to produce new media arts works that infuse their ideas and interests. Therefore, new forms of expression emerge at the intersection of youth's cultural practices in digital media and the professional skills and processes offered at the programs explored. The curricula offered at all the sites are neither overly prescriptive nor unstructured. Instead, there was a unique space in which participants could playfully explore ideas, issues, and interests within a structure that taught them how to give form to their varied artistic inquiries.

Within the context of professional learning communities, programs like Frames (Chapter 2) and GIFTS (Chapter 5) create spaces for students to play, imagine, and experiment, while having the support of professionals guiding them through a filmmaking methodology. This is similar

DOI: 10.1057/9781137475176.0010

to both of the school film programs studied by Black in Chapter 4. In her analysis, she concludes that students' creative productions are derived from their experiences, all the while supported with a professional film-making environment. And as explored in Chapter 3, students at Maison Kekpart are openly encouraged to share their digital cultural practices in social media and taught through example and practice to develop a professional identity online. As Lin argues in Chapter 2, the interplay between digital media and creativity is not only to prepare young people for job-readiness under the impact of an economic rationale for learning, but it indicates new models of social and cultural practices that foreground engagement, collaboration, and dialogue. We observed that each learning community flourishes in spaces where students' cultural practices and interests are valued and transformed through artistic explorations.

Pedagogy of new media art education

To create a space in which youth can introduce their ideas into a structure based on professional new media practices, teachers must be flexible. The adaptability that educators and teachers exercise in their pedagogical practice is often observed as acting as a problem solver for students. Teachers and educators create a safe space where students articulate ideas and they respond by pointing out possibilities and pitfalls in the process of production. The instructors observed and interviewed in each chapter followed their students' ideas and sought to give the tools and methods for youths' personal expression as professionals. The instructors afford students the space for youths to playfully explore ideas within a structure that supports their artistic outcomes.

Key to the creation of a flexible and creative space are the quality of relationships between students and teachers. What characterizes such relationships is a fluid hierarchy, where at one moment teachers hold ultimate responsibility to ensure student safety while also flattening their power relationship with students in the production of new media art. Oftentimes in the eyes of students their teachers act as consultants on their projects by offering expertise on an ad hoc basis. The result is meaningful learning because it arises from the needs and goals determined by students. Further, teachers achieve this leveling of relationships with students by placing the onus on students to be responsible to

DOI: 10.1057/9781137475176.0010

the work, rather than working for grades or teacher's expectations. The demonstration of such relationships has been exhibited many times by creating an event or venue for students' work to be disseminated in film festivals, public screenings, or exhibitions. The instructors would use these external commitments as motivation for students to work through the process. The shifting of responsibility, from the teacher to the work itself, enabled teachers and students to work together through the process using each phase to teach and learn from each other.

To enable this comfort and trust in the process, teachers in all of the new media programs studied in this book have professional experience that they draw from in the setup, design, and implementation of their respective programs. Students recognize that their instructors have expertise through instructors' willingness to teach and structure their pedagogy and curricula as if they are actually on a professional new media arts production team. In Chapter 4, Black describes the varied professional backgrounds of the instructors studied and how their experiences complement their colleague's skills and experiences. At GIFTS, described in Chapter 5, instructors would often work as professional film and television actors, directors, and sound designers and teach in-between projects. The Frames program, highlighted in Chapter 2, similarly has new media professionals teaching youth. And at Maison Kekpart, new media artists are instructors who invite students into their professional networks through social media so that youths can see firsthand how their educators network and disseminate their professional productions.

When the teachers we observed and interviewed encounter a limit in their professional knowledge, they do not hesitate to seek expert knowledge within and beyond the program. At GIFTS, a team of instructors are responsible for guiding groups through the week-long process of making a film. The teams are constituted of film directors, actors, film editors, and camera and sound technicians. At the two school programs described in Chapter 4 by Black, local professionals in the community are often invited into schools to teach specific aspects of their craft. Likewise the same tack is taken by educators at Frames in Vancouver and Maison Kekpart in Montreal. Entrenched in the pedagogical practice of teachers is the notion that they do not hold all of the knowledge. Consequently, educators model for students the proactive measures of soliciting those who do have the expertise to consult with and ask to contribute to their learning. For teachers in these programs, this is an

DOI: 10.1057/9781137475176.0010

essential part of their pedagogical and professional practice. Admitting and even embracing that they, as educators, do not know everything and demonstrating professional networking and resourcefulness emphasizes the flattened relationships of power between teachers and students and thus shifts the emphasis of responsibility to the work itself.

Connecting curricula to the larger community

Bringing in and incorporating new media professionals from the local community into the curriculum requires an acknowledgment of the importance of connecting what the students learn and do to the larger community, outside of the educational context. As mentioned earlier, incorporating professionals into ad hoc teaching roles signals to the students that knowledge is distributed among many in a community of professionals and that being fluent in new media arts production is not just knowing how to use a specific technology or process but also being able to identify and utilize knowledge resources. Critical to being a successful new media artist is cultivating a network of knowledge expertise from which one can draw upon to meet specific aspects of the project.

Not only do members of the community play a role in the production undertaken in these programs, but the larger community becomes the destination for the students' new media works. Again, teachers refer to the community not only as an endpoint or audience where work is eventually disseminated, but also they illuminate community with the intention of motivating their students to feel accountable to larger audiences. At GIFTS, a large wooden clock delineates each phase of the film workshop, which culminates with a public screening of students' work. Similarly, Frames culminates workshops for youth with public screenings. In Chapter 4, Black describes how both public school programs use film festivals, public screenings, and social media to motivate students to both complete large-scale projects and engage the public with their ideas. Likewise for Maison Kekpart, the use of social media is seen as an essential tool to teach youth how to engage with the public and build their professional network.

Educators and administrators across the new media arts programs featured in this book all recognize the need to think of their educational contexts as broader than the walls of the school or community center. For

DOI: 10.1057/9781137475176.0010

them, the building is just the hub that is placed within a more extensive network of pedagogical relationships. Teaching and learning relationships are redefined in these spaces and rely heavily on wider community involvement and support. Connecting with the public outside of schools and community centers enables students in these programs to see their contributions as not simply fulfilling an assignment, but rather as more significantly making a contribution to the cultural life of their communities. And for the educators and administrators, being an active and visible presence in the community generates support, both financially and politically, for their programs.

Creating the conditions for youth engagement

The challenges that formal and informal learning environments face are distinctly different. On the one hand, in formal settings teachers and students are held to a different level of governmental policy and regulation, while informal contexts have, on the surface, the level of flexibility not readily available in most public schools. On the other hand, administrators and educators of informal contexts are continually seeking external funding and support to fulfill their missions. Regardless of the kinds of challenges each program faces, what they have in common is adaptable, flexible leadership that actively seeks to create the conditions for innovative curricula and pedagogy described in this book. Both educators and administrators in formal and informal sites play leadership roles in each of the programs described. The defining quality of leadership across contexts is best described as creating the conditions for engagement in youth.

Situations of commitment are manifested in differing ways depending on the challenges faced and the local context. For educators in these new media programs, they create the conditions for engagement by producing curricula that are driven by students' ideas and concerns, while also providing a clear methodology for professional new media arts production. They are advocates for their students' and their creative works while navigating the educational systems. Instructor's leadership qualities resemble that of film producers as they ensure the right equipment, skills, and roles are in place before and during production. Additionally, for administrators we observed that they create the conditions and support for educators to engage in the activities described by adapting the

DOI: 10.1057/9781137475176.0010

structures and resources to serve youth best. This is abundantly apparent in the two public school programs in Chapter 4. The administrators in each school afford unusual flexibility and autonomy to the educators involved. These administrators do not take a hands-off approach, but rather they actively engage in understanding and supporting the goals of educators and their teaching in these programs. While administrators in informal learning settings have less governmental regulation than in formal settings, they have to contend with varied and sporadic in funding sources. Much of their time is spent building partnerships in the community with other nonprofit organizations, pubic institutions, and corporations. For example, administrators at Frog Hollow (Chapter 2) and Maison Kekpart (Chapter 3) strategically use the neoliberal economic justification to solicit funding and justify their existence to the public. It's a delicate relationship among funders, administrators, and the public. The challenges that administrators face from both informal and formal learning environments are varied in reacting to the changing landscape of learning with digital media for younger generations. Such challenges also provoke educators and administrators to rethink and reconceptualize notions such as creativity, relationship, identity, professionalism, and community with an underlying orientation toward ensuring the success of their educators and students.

At the conclusion of Chapter 1, we posed a number of questions that are themed around youth cultural practices within both formal and informal contexts. What we concluded is that there is more that connects innovative and successful informal and formal new media arts programs for youth than separates them. There is an underlying assumption, that given the increasing standardization of formal education, creative innovation is most likely to occur in informal settings. Instead, we have discovered that innovation in new media arts education can flourish in formal educational settings as well as in informal contexts. These programs flourish through a determined yet flexible leadership with a clear vision of who they serve and how best to support youth in learning. It is our aim that this book serves as an alternative discourse by presenting compelling cases that share a set of distinguishing characteristics that engage youth in creative new media arts practices regardless of institutional structures. What is clear to us is that what educators and administrators have to learn from the programs presented in this book is that, further discussion, strong leadership, and a determination to be flexible in these changing times

DOI: 10.1057/9781137475176.0010

for both educators and administrators in formal and informal learning environments will ultimately determine the success of any new media educational endeavor.

Reference

Sefton-Green, J. (2014). From "othering" to incorporation: the dilemmas of crossing informal and formal learning boundaries. In K. Sanford, T. Rogers, & M. Kendrick (Eds), *Everyday Youth Literacies: Critical Perspectives for New Times* (pp. 175–189). Singapore: Springer.

DOI: 10.1057/9781137475176.0010

Index

DOI: 10.1057/9781137475176.0011

DOI: 10.1057/9781137475176.0011

DOI: 10.1057/9781137475176.0011

GPSR Compliance
The European Union's (EU) General Product Safety Regulation (GPSR) is a set of rules that requires consumer products to be safe and our obligations to ensure this.

If you have any concerns about our products, you can contact us on

ProductSafety@springernature.com

In case Publisher is established outside the EU, the EU authorized representative is:

Springer Nature Customer Service Center GmbH
Europaplatz 3
69115 Heidelberg, Germany

www.ingramcontent.com/pod-product-compliance
Lightning Source LLC
LaVergne TN
LVHW091519200926
848483LV00002B/256
* 9 7 8 1 1 3 7 4 7 5 1 6 9 *